Reality and Theatre

Reality

Naim Kattan

and Theatre

translated from the French by Alan Brown

Anansi

Le Réel et le Théatral was first published in 1970 by Editions HMH, 380 ouest, rue Craig, Montréal. It was published in Paris by Editions Grasset in 1971. French text copyright Editions HMH.

This translation was completed with the assistance of the Province of Ontario Council for the Arts.

Cover design by Frank Loconte.

ISBN: 0 88784 710 2 (cloth)
Library of Congress Card Number: 74-190702

Printed in Canada by The Hunter Rose Company.

House of Anansi Press
471 Jarvis Street
Toronto 284, Canada

Table of Contents

Preface

Do we know what an Iraqi thinks? Or even how he thinks? Where, for that matter, is Iraq? Where is our cradle? Where did man learn to live in history, and to think in the true sense of the word (i.e., to write)? Naim Kattan comes from there, and few will welcome what he has to say.

Our society loves protesters: they are its heroes and its conscience. Naim Kattan does not protest: he observes. He does not argue, he looks, and sees our manners and our idols. Our society would swallow the logic of an academic or make parlour games out of some amateur's complex and ingenious analysis. It revels in playing intellectual hide-and-seek, but it cannot tolerate being *seen*.

What we have in this book is not the noisy revolt of a schoolboy, the massive dissertation of an intellectual, nor the casual essay of a dilettante. Naim Kattan banks his fires. Sober, restrained, without flourish and even without system, unless we mean the system of the ancestors of the human mind, his gaze reaches us from the depths of the ages, challenging what we call the process of thinking, particularly as we apply it to ourselves: the mental and visceral structures of our respective tribes, structures from which there is no escape, whether through individualism or universalism.

He does not think us as we think ourselves, but neither is he the prisoner of some far Tierra del Fuego, nor the simple "peasant from the Danube." He resembles civilisation itself, true civilisation, of the kind that preceded rhetoric and Greek logic and all the supposedly poetical or philosophical embellishments that have since become their trappings. In his book the Frankish phrase, with its traditional and modern neatness, joins the ancient genius of Akkad. The mind's movement consists precisely of this alternate hammering by the great smiths, and their juxtaposition at the dawn of history led to those marvellous achievements of which certain obscure nations have not yet perceived the glow.

Here, in fact, is a book whose every page gives a new landscape as setting to the same ever-novel experience. Its light is often cruel when it probes our hidden places, clarifying the confrontations of centuries and continents, exposing our souls, our wars, our cities, our literature, politics and science. But what freedom, finally, from accepted myths and notions, and what a preparation — after so many false starts — for a true departure!

Jean Grosjean

Reality and Theatre

Introduction

∧ Who receives the applause at the end of a play? The actors? the author? And for what reason? The pleasure given? the amusement? the quality of emotion aroused and experienced? Does the public in this vibrant hall suspect that its enthusiasm is motivated by more than gratitude or pleasure? The act of clapping loudly involves more than the hands: the whole body participates, and in this I see a desire to put an end to a state of mind, to signal the close of an episode. The borderline of the theatrical has to be drawn, especially when its effect has been devastatingly strong. The physical fact of clapping would be absurd if it did not signal a return to reality. Hands clap, and everyday life reasserts itself.

It was in Paris that I saw my first play. Baghdad, where I was born, is (like all the oriental cities I have known or visited) a spectacle in itself. When I was a child there was not a theatre in the city. But bargaining in a bazaar was a kind of play in which everyone was actor and spectator at once. The scope of this play is purposely limited, for it consists of everyday acts, not matters of life or death. Love, death and honour are too serious to be reduced to a game. Reality is used up in daily life. The project does not inhibit spontaneity, it is prolonged in a succession of spontaneities. What is theatrical here is a part of the movement of life, and cannot be circumscribed, isolated or recognised as a category or mode in itself. An integral part of daily behaviour, theatre has no borderlines, and by this fact loses its role as a distinct element of civilisation.

It was because theatre was a part of my way of being, an everyday fact, that I was able to appreciate the extent to which it forms the base of western life. For daily life to be theatre, as in the East, each man must possess the power to be himself and the other, actor and spectator, native and foreigner. There is no separation of these roles, for each character is separated within himself. Who, then, is better qualified than an Oriental, not to observe or understand or conceive the West, but to experience and enter it without losing himself, or to adopt it without dissolving his own identity? Thus, I experienced the East and West in succession, and then simultaneously; and I learned that, if we succeed in understanding what is not exhausted in spontaneity, if we can observe from the outside the multiple spectacle of the world, we transform into theatre what was not felt instantaneously. And because the instantaneous is open to doubling of roles, we can multiply ourselves without loss of self. Of course I can not speak of what I have not experienced in at least a fleeting, episodic way. I have never been in China, or India, or Japan, and when I use the word "Orient" I mean the one I bear within me, the Semitic East. I have seen Kabuki and No dramas. For me these are facts of civilisation that I can observe or study, but to speak of them here would be to place them at two removes from reality, for they are already at one remove by the mere fact of being spectacles. Does this mean that one can only speak of what one has experienced in a personal way? Yes, to the extent that one refuses to be limited by theatre, that is to say by the concept. What we are talking about is a peculiarly artistic experience that is at the same time participation and detachment; for every artist is at once actor and spectator.

In Europe my malaise was that of the Orient suddenly projected into the world of the machine. Life in the East exhausts itself in its own movement, and the world serves as an instrument to satisfy sensuality. Theatre is not detached from experience, and spontaneity absorbs all available energy. All works are ephemeral, and the only monuments are the family house and the house of God, Who is also the god of communal solidarity. Literature is a celebration of life

3

and its creator, and art is an ornament to the habitat man carves out of nature with God's approval. The malaise of the East comes from its inability to separate theatre from life, to make of it a structure, a category apart. Because I was accustomed to a daily theatre of life which I experienced and observed simultaneously, I was able to appreciate the strength of the West, where I found myself in the midst of a multiple theatre. Here a thousand intermediaries were set up to link man to reality, and when the intermediary, grown all-powerful, replaced reality, I saw the West trapped in its own system. I am irresistibly drawn to this magnetic universe with its seductive multiplicity, but just at the point of being absorbed and swallowed by it I draw back: the actor doubles his function, I become a spectator. I have one foot in each world, I have only to shift and it is the East that becomes a spectacle for me. This movement to and fro, this perpetual change of viewpoint, is to say the least uncomfortable, unless I recognise in it what is the true virtue of the East, the lesson I carry with me as a secular heritage: the spectator is an actor who is himself a spectator. . . . If one does not become the victim of this perpetual movement, which can easily turn into an idle game, one can live in two worlds without being torn between them. The observer is lucid; he is detached, but his detachment is momentary and his lucidity is grave.

For me to understand the West I must not allow its theatre to impose the role of spectator on me. In other words, I refuse the status of foreigner. I have absorbed this theatre and experienced its various aspects; first of all, language, which penetrates all the others. As a child I had already learned to establish my distance from words. They already had a double existence for me. My written language was not the one I spoke. In French every word became for me an apprenticeship and a conquest. This tongue which I acquired forced me each day to reformulate my duality and my identity. In the process identity became an act of life, a daily discovery.

4

My dreams and my childhood have been metamorphosed, and no longer serve me as a reference point. The
present can also not be taken for granted. I can not recover
the innocence of an experience at whose birth I was not
present. Conscious reflection has taken over, and each word
marks daily life with its own weight. Knowledge precedes
innocence, and allows it to be reborn in a second innocence. I
am a bearer of the word, and subject to it. It is a possession
and a force which are external to me. The word is habitat to
me, the foreigner. It bestows on me a second self. I set up
against it a language already metamorphosed, which springs
from a buried universe and makes me spectator of the new
language that is defining and reconstructing me. The word is
doubled: it is light and it is reflection. I am witness to my
own actions, I take them by surprise in their spontaneity.
Could I live now without being spectator of my own life?
Nothing is completely exhausted in the instantaneous. I
understand now that all art is an attack on life, for it is the
product of life made motionless. If it intervenes after the
fact, if it follows life's exhaustion, this is only in order to
delay its new beginning. The West is inhabited by art because
the West's way of conjuring death is to install it at the heart
of life. To pursue permanence or immortality is to refuse
nature, which is fleeting and spontaneous. It is an attempt to
stop all movement. But we need to be in the midst of
movement, we must be at once its motor and its spectator, if
art is to be a true conjuration of death and not a second,
ersatz life. If art refers only to itself, if immobility becomes
an end in itself, if art is no longer a mediation with reality, it
is dissipated in a futile, desperate and gratuitous game.

The world does not exist to answer our needs and
desires. Nature exists in its own right, but when man affirms
his presence he submits to the presence of nature and
constructs a second nature depicting a life that goes beyond
the span of his own. The monuments of art are no more than
a desperate attempt at permanence or immortality. When we
detach ourselves from the globe we inhabit we transform it

5

into decor, and the city becomes a theatre where man is the spectator of his own immortality. The city should be demolished and rebuilt in a continuous process, to the extent that the theatre it constitutes ceases to inspire confidence or the spectator ceases to be convinced. If this is not done the city is no longer a mediation with reality or an extension of it, but an autonomous theatre that whittles away reality while annihilating man. When one is not occupying a city there is no end to the reconstruction needed to complete its conquest. The need for reconstruction escapes the spectator who is reduced to a single view. He is no longer the master of his own word, unless he is an artist capable of slicing out of the spontaneity of experience a portion which he immobilises in death. This pursuit of the work, this life snatched from death and handed to the artist, is carried on at what price? What is left to the artist but his own immobility in silence, his resignation to fate? For one who changes worlds and refuses exile is there any condition but that of artist, unless he accepts his own disappearance into a world of shadows? He lives a double life, building it into a work of which he becomes the spectator once his original spontaneity has been recovered. And if he comes from the Orient to the West, the latter will no longer be an enigma to him, because he experiences it from within and observes it from without, exactly as an artist lives and observes his works.

It was in Europe that I discovered a new sensuality. Coming from a society where woman is kept at a distance I discovered her as an image, for beauty held is never conquered. I contemplated her, and became her spectator. There were the most varied stimulants to looking. At the beginning this distant woman seemed superior to the one whose odour can also be perceived. Like a city in which I am tourist and constructor, woman became that part of myself which I explored at leisure, which died and was reborn every moment and whose permanence lay in alternation, in the exhaustion of experience. There is a constant temptation to linger over the image, to be content with seeing and no more.

6

In this case one is imprisoned within the spectacle, and the only remaining choice is experimentation in sensuality, indicating despair at always finding oneself on the threshold of an unattainable reality. Here again I refused the role of foreigner, refused to be an exile from myself. One can, of course, take refuge in morality, an illusory consolation. In a world of mirrors morality tries to preserve the possibility of reality by condemning its expression, accepting the pretence that the image is reality's reflection.

The West revealed to me my own double nature. To resist comfortable pigeon-holing and avoid inner conflict one chooses immobility. I resisted definitions and categories, though they are most useful for classifying the dead and tracing the frontiers of graveyards. I did not want to be burdened with them from the start, did not want the movement of daily life to be predictable and thus nullified. Rigorous intellectual discipline seemed to me an admirable theatre. It gave the impression of continuing the movement of reality when it had in fact ceased, and thus made death the most distinguished expression of life. If one wants at all costs to avoid inner conflict one becomes prey to a tottering between violence and annihilation. I learned that contradictions can be resolved only at the expense of everyday life. All passion becomes a refusal when it sets itself up as a pre-defined absolute. Can I preserve the East without reducing it to exoticism or nostalgia? Can I accept the West without making into an ethic my fears of the dangers it contains, without making a moral principle of my resistance to annihilation? There is no method but that of daily life in all its anarchy. Every identity is born of a constant confrontation between motion and immobility. It was in the West, of all places, that I was able to experience the Orient, welcoming the new contingencies of a strange world where I felt at ease; each world became for the other a threat and a safeguard, weaving in a perpetual motion an identity which was open but never clearly defined. The West, transported into the Orient, becomes pure theatre, and in the process

7

makes theatre of an Orient which is reduced to nothingness. In the West the Orient is no more than a subject for study, exotic and at best provocative of nostalgia. The true Orient must be an inner fact, lived out daily, not in order to refuse the West but to tame it and transform its theatre into reality. Otherwise it is an exile, and creates the condition of the indifferent spectator in a theatre to which he does not give his recognition. The persistence of the East can transform the West into a work of art. I rediscover in daily life the relationship of the artist to reality, carving his work out of life, which in its turn is formulated by his work.

To be a Jew and an Arab, and to experience this conflict as an aberration, an illness . . . I refuse as foreign to me the contradiction which denies the movement of life and opens the door to a violence that spells doom for two uncertain cultures. I refuse to be imprisoned in this war, this oscillation between a reality that cannot be lived and a theatre that cannot be mastered. And what if I were forced to live in the heart of this conflict, if the uncauterised wound were thrust on me every day, if there were no way out? Theatre would then have such force that no reality could resist it. I am not trying on the pose of wisdom. I experience this madness from afar and observe it, and my detachment is not the result of distance. In the blind passion of taking sides I discern a refusal of uncomfortable uncertainties. Must the gestures of everyday be sacrificed to the deceptive warmth of a theatrical communion? The only fidelity is that which is subject to perpetual rebirth through daily life, obeying the dictates of a reality buried in ambiguity and confusion.

The time is past when, in an Orient subjected to the cruelty of nature and the caprice of princes, the meander of daily life could somehow be identified with that of reality. The time is past when, in an Occident no less subject to nature and the will of monarchs, an effective theatre allowed mediation between man and reality. Now that in both worlds the frontiers of reality and theatre are blurred, certainties crumble, and all that is left is the uncertain movement of a fragile everyday life. Now the theatre, having lost its mediating virtue, becomes an instrument of enquiry and exploration. By accepting the dramatisations of the West and obeying its theatre I can withdraw to a point where a few feeble rays of reality become visible. And the theatre, creator of works of art, permits a double role, allows me to safeguard the fragile expression of a fusion with the world: an experience of reality without mediation. Momentary absence from the self, welcoming of the other self, become oppressive when one of the two selves proclaims its victory over uncertainty, putting reality to flight along with all contingencies. The day of global truth and unities is over, unless one chooses totalitarianism and death. On the other hand, perpetual doubt is yet another highly theatrical illusion. What must be sought is a constant involvement in daily life. Detachment is a necessary step leading to this involvement, which in its turn leads back to detachment, in an acceptance of perpetual alternation between the theatrical and the real, which are nourished by their mutual contact and re-created by each other. It is easy to condemn this attitude as playing the waiting game. For me it is a way of joining the world, founding myself in its movement without losing myself in its theatre. It is also a way of making two universes cohabit within me without making the final choice that would condemn one or the other to assimilation. It is a way of preserving a field of being, however limited, for reality. Is this not a way to liberty? Even if the way is less than sure. . . .

Reality and Theatre

While Greek civilization found its highest expression in drama, the Semitic world never knew this form of art. Dramatists had no place in either Arab or Hebrew literature. In recent generations, of course, national theatres have developed in the countries of the Middle-East, but they spring from western influences assimilated and adapted to present-day needs. Even the novel is almost totally absent in the civilization of the Middle-East. There are two exceptions, and important ones at that: the sacred narrative, whether we mean the Bible or the Koran, and the popular tale – which the cultural elite considered a vulgar product, not fit to be classed as literature. An example is the *Thousand and One Nights.* There have been, to be sure, borrowings from foreign civilizations throughout Arab history; but when the caliphs of Baghdad and Damascus invited Greek culture and its living representatives into their palaces, they made a choice. It was the scientists, the philosophers and historians they summoned, never the dramatists. And when the stories resembling the fables of Aesop (such as Kulaila and Dimna) were introduced into Arab literature, they were of foreign origin, and intended mainly for children.

We are faced with the question of why the art of drama found no adepts in the Arab and Jewish civilizations. It would be frivolous to explain this fact by an absence of creative talent or men of genius, for both civilizations are there for us to see and both have produced – in other domains – the talent needed to create what has been accomplished. The reason is to be found elsewhere. It lies in the very basis of the Semitic civilizations.

Every civilization is launched and developed according to fundamental options and choices. There are three kinds of relationships involved: those of man with nature, those that govern his contacts with other men, and those he establishes with the beyond. The split between the Semitic East and the Hellenic West is to be found in their divergent notions of the relation of man to nature. In Greece, nature enveloped man, surrounding him with her benefits, but also with her threats. She might on occasion seem hostile, but well-being and happiness had their source in her all-pervading presence. The logical and predictable consequence was the divinisation of nature. The Greek gods were masters of the elements, they granted their blessings to men, and protected them from the dangers of the forces the gods controlled.

In the Eastern desert, nature was the enemy, the hostile force from which man needed constant protection. The moment God made Abraham the father of monotheism, he led him from his desert toward a more hospitable land. All nomads dreamed of this promised land, this refuge offered by God as a reward, this dreamland, flowing with milk and honey. But nature in this benevolent and happy form could not be deified, for it belonged to a dream which only hidden forces from another sphere could offer as a reward.

The forty years which the Jews spend in the desert transform the dream into an expectation, and their alliance with the one God puts within their reach a nature in which years of famine do not follow years of plenty.

As soon as Mohammed had broken the idols from which his own tribe, Quraych, drew its authority, and transformed the Kaaba from a pagan meeting-ground into a holy place of the one God, the point of departure was there, and Arabs poured out of the desert to conquer green fields and river-valleys.

For the Semite, nature is not a blind force which one need only tame and domesticate in order to obtain her blessings. It is the hostile terrain from which one must flee in order to conquer the right to live. For the Greek, life belongs

11

to the elements. The forces of nature and the vital forces of man can be at one. In the Semite's desert, life asserts itself against nature by outwitting the elements, by fleeing from its perils, its aridity, by searching for other landscapes, gentler climates. From this starting-point the relationship of man to man is also determined. The tribe is grouped in an alliance for survival through collective strength. It breaks down not only the obstacles raised by nature, but also those created by the existence of other tribes.

Nature is not a refuge, it is the common enemy. The struggle is not to establish man within it, but to escape it altogether. Life is certainly as sacred in the East as in the West; but while the Greeks proclaimed the sacred character of life by sacralising nature, the Semites defined the sacred not in relation to nature but in relation to the one and only superior force: that of the beyond.

Instead of the forces of that other sphere combining with nature against man, it is man who allies himself with God, if not to control nature at least to ward off its perils. This relationship is manifest in the languages themselves. In Hebrew and Arabic there is no separation between words and things. The object lives because it is named. The problem which still exists for Western poets in our day was solved from the beginning in the Biblical and Koranic languages. Things are not qualified, much less made abstract. They are said. If Arabic has several hundred names for the sword, the horse, the camel or the lion, it is because each name designates a particular state of being. Instead of qualifying an animal, we re-name it. Its size and colour are not indicated by adjectives, they are implicit in its name.

This identity of word and thing expresses the relationship of man and reality. In the Greek world, reality is exterior to man, separate, possessing its own dimension. Such is not the case in the Semitic world. Western man, a product of the Hellenic tradition, needs an intermediary, a conductor,

12

to establish his contact with reality. The concept allows him to establish a rapport between a thought and an action which are otherwise discrete.

In the same way the theatre creates a bridge between emotion and lived reality. Western man is, as a result, a man divided, of two minds, and the alienation of the twentieth century is merely the culminating form of a dichotomy that began with the Greeks.

We are not, of course, talking about a rigid division. In the Semitic world the tendencies that won out in Greece have also played their role, often a decisive one. In Greece the quest for unity persisted even in periods when the theatre was triumphant. There are two contrary tendencies giving rise to tensions and ambiguities, often even direct confrontations.

When Judaism reached the phase of constructing an organized society, the Law removed the elements of anarchy implicit in man's direct relationship with God, and in his relationship with reality. The gift of nature's benefits was conditional on obedience to this Law, and any breach was followed by punishment (in particular by the forty years of wandering and waiting in the desert). Later, the prophets reminded kings of the true meaning of rapport with reality. The City itself must be made a sacred place if the promise was to be fulfilled and the City was to endure. The condition of its endurance was perpetual renewal. This ideal city never materialized, but the dream of its coming never disappeared. Through the centuries there was always a minority who believed the marriage of ideal and reality to be no dream but a promise. Promise or dream, this ideal Orient was constantly awaited.

Christianity was transformed the moment it left the shores of the Jordan River. From its oriental home it carried a fundamental attitude to life, which had to be protected against the threat of nature. The Miracle multiplies loaves and

13

fishes. But at the same time Christianity absorbs (and transforms) the western attitude to life. Death becomes not a termination but a point of departure. Man's triumph is his power of resurrection. He refuses nature its victory, for death is transfigured and becomes a source of life. Christianity is not, like primal Judaism, a denial of theatre; it is a transfiguration of theatre.

With Islam the process is quite different. Its point of departure was also the Judaism of the desert, the marriage of man to reality. But the result is not a daily rebirth. In Islam man submits to reality (the word *aslama* means "has submitted"). Reality is inscribed in history, and man, in submitting to it, conquers nature and reality by the mark he makes on the course of history. The relationship with reality is no longer individualistic and anarchical; it is collective, and accepts the passage of time.

For both these worlds, the Jews represented the untiring expectation of the primal Orient. What could seem more strange in the West, an amalgam of Nordic paganism and Roman organization, than this little group proclaiming the primacy of the One, and rejecting all theatre, even sacred theatre?

European antisemitism is a rejection of the primal Orient. In rejecting the Jews, the Christians of Rome in fact rejected the Eastern basis of their religion. Later, when a foreign and redoubtable Orient was close and victorious, when the Arabs imposed their reign in the West, the fear of Semitism took on a more concrete aspect. To preserve the kind of balance which theatre made possible in the West, Europe had to be freed from the Orient. The struggle was most bitter in Spain. And when the Spanish monarchs expelled their Orientals, they made little distinction between Jew and Moslem.

But the experience of the wedding of man with reality leaves its mark. Spain never quite recovered from its exposure to the Orient, though the version to which Spain was exposed may have fallen short of the oriental ideal. Spain continued in South America the inscription in history that was part of the process of Islam. And the theatrical, in this Spain, assumed some most original forms. The corrida pushes play to the frontiers of reality. Life, in the shedding of blood, touches death, and reality is vanquished by theatre. At the other extreme, Don Quixote is tragic because he fails to provide a bridge between man and reality. Don Quixote appears to us pathetic and ridiculous because he dreams of attaining reality while confusing it with the theatrical.

For the Jews of Eastern Europe the Orient has remained their unrealized dream. Even in Yiddish literature of recent times we find Isaac Bashevis Singer describing (in his novel *The Ram's Horn*) the consternation aroused in a little Polish village by the appearance in the Orient of the false Messiah, Chabatai Ben Zvi. And certain orthodox Jews in Poland described their ritual as Sephardic. Christians, for their part, were conscious of this persistence of the East in the heart of Europe. For Walter Scott, Rebecca is oriental, and Balzac's Jewish characters belong, by virtue of their expression and features, to a distant Orient.

The ultimate in western theatricality was doubtless Nazism itself, and its most redoubtable enemy appeared in the guise of the Jew. This form of theatricality was no longer a bridge between man and reality, it was the negation of man and of reality itself. The West itself, of course, and not only among the Jews of Europe, has never quite given up the search for an ideal Orient whose nature and even origin it has long forgotten. Periodically poets and artists testify to the persistence of this ideal. The automatism of the surrealists surely amounts to such a testimony, though they were influenced at the same time by centuries of Hellenistic conceptualization and contemporary Freudianism.

The Jews have attempted, at times freely and at times under bitter pressure, to preserve their ancestral heritage while assimilating the contributions of the time. Is not Hassidism a kind of adaptation of Russian mysticism? And is not the Haskala the extrapolation of the revolutions of Europe?

The monotheistic Orient never succeeded in a total abolition of its various paganisms. Moreover, the crushing triumphs of Christianity and Islam made Jews for centuries forget their original expectations. The fact that the Promised Land is extended to include the whole earth does not change its nature. And the conquest of reality by submission to history has given place to the rise of mercantile and, finally, industrial Europe. The Jews, in their most tragic periods, continued to proclaim the future coming of a primal, never-accomplished unity. And the other Semite, the Arab, has taken the road of creating his Orient within himself.

For centuries Christianity was the only theatre of the Occident — and most often an imperceptible one. Man's contact with the two realities (the earth and the beyond) was achieved by the expedient of faith. The Middle Ages were its climax, its apogee and the beginning of its decline.

Any lucid reflection on a situation is proof of a certain detachment towards it. The Christians of the Middle Ages, when they talked of their faith, proclaimed their devotion and satisfaction. But in the very act of doing so they expressed a shade of doubt and nostalgia. The spontaneity was broken. And it was at this point that theatre reappeared. The mystery-plays had as their sole purpose the confirmation of a rapport with reality. But through them the sacred theatre descended into the street. It left behind the protective walls of churches and set itself up on their porches and squares. This act was an implicit recognition of a need which faith no longer satisfied. The theatre, moreover, could not indefinitely conserve its sacred character. As cities

16

developed, as kingdoms took root and society grew more diversified, secularization became more common and the profane nature of a great part of the collective life became obvious.

In *Life is a Dream,* Calderon cast doubt on the very existence of reality. In a way he thus gave the theatre a new function: to reveal the unceasing quest for a renewed relationship with reality.

In Shakespeare, and later in Molière, the theatre did not merely take itself for granted; it proclaimed itself as a necessity. If the world is theatre, the dramatist, searching out its secrets, reveals a hidden or shadowed reality. The relationship of man to man is theatrical, and as a result the theatre is no longer a play of masks but truth itself.

Molière explores the precise meaning of social relationships by exposing the subtle interplays arbitrarily elaborated by a society incapable of establishing an authentic relationship with reality. When he introduces pairs of couples, echoing the masked antics of the masters in the servants' hall, or when he brings into play the differences between generations, Molière is trying to reflect a reality in the process of disintegration: a social reality that cannot be reconstructed and come into its own unless it is dominated by the will and freedom of the individual.

Marivaux goes further. Words and phrases are used not to coincide with things or even to hint at things, but to conceal them. The more consciously and willingly the theatre chooses to become a screen, the more it is compelled to rediscover the authentic. Marivaux shows us that the most subtle and most perfectly contrived theatre is inadequate because it obscures instead of furthering the relationship between man and reality. This kind of theatre is carried to an extreme in the plays of Musset. Here we see a breakthrough of the individual's will to impose his need for renewed relationships in order to be freed from the theatricality that infests society. This will asserts itself and receives dramatic

17

setbacks in Kleist's *Prince of Homburg,* and in *Danton's Death* by Büchner.

———————————

It is significant that the adolescent figures so widely in romantic literature. There is a parallel between the Western adolescent's attitude to reality and the prevailing theatricality.

Adolescence, as we know it, is a recent invention. It is one that is eminently western. The Jewish child in fact takes on the responsibilities of adulthood when he becomes a Bar Mitzvah at the age of thirteen. He becomes a member of the community, and his actions count for something in it. In Arab culture in the Middle East the child passed directly to adulthood until schools were established in cities and study became an intermediate step.

In the western world a man's entry on stage is held back, and the period of waiting is called adolescence. But the problem goes beyond the sociological. In classical times a young man waited for permission from his elders to take his place in the world that was reserved for them. The romantic adolescent's attitude is quite the reverse. He refuses to accept rules of the game imposed by a well-established society. He becomes a threat to its very foundations, and the theatre which that society has created in its own image loses its power. The adolescent asserts his individual autonomy. He proclaims his right to contrive his own theatre. He most certainly has no desire to take his place in the adult world; in fact, he rejects it completely. The theatrical is not for him the bridge that leads to adulthood. His loathing is all-embracing, it takes in the whole of reality. His own theatricality thus becomes an effort to unleash the Dionysiac power of the individual. It is at once a rejection and an affirmation, a defiant presence and a panic flight.

Stendhal gives implicit recognition to the failure of this romantic stance. Fabrice del Dongo strolls through the

18

battlefield of Waterloo. He is aware of events, but decides to pass them by. His attitude is not one of rejection or flight, but of the assumption of a mask. His relationship with reality does not take the form of confrontation or refusal. It is an oblique relationship. The adolescent hero becomes aware of his own inadequacy, and though he makes a pretence of gaiety he is nonetheless somewhere on the fringes of madness.

Beginning with the Renaissance the theatre grew more diversified in the western world. Classical French theatre becomes a second reality which informs, describes or modifies primary reality. The characters of Racine or Corneille represent man situated beyond contingencies. Reality is reduced to its essentials and the relationship of man with himself and others transcends the everyday, goes beyond the single event.

Shakespearian theatre has a totally different point of departure. Here the particular, the contingent and the concrete are the components of reality. This reality is seized and transcended through the use of no ingredients other than its own substance. The Shakespearian hero lives in the world and its events, and it is via the particular that he sums up human experience.

Two theatres, and as a result two indirect relationships with reality.

The Italians developed a theatre which places them on the fringe of the Orient. In their case there was no direct confrontation with the East, such as we witnessed in Spain. The relationship of Italians to the Orient was created according to conditions laid down by the Italians themselves. To explore the individual conscience and its relationships with social reality, the Commedia dell' Arte presents us with a second reality — a theatrical one, consisting of a convention, a game whose rules must be accepted by all concerned. The characters are not transformed by the actors and we find no trace of philosophy or psychology. This second reality is not a pointless game. It is, in fact, a representation of life as it is. The masks are not related to the situation of the game beyond time and space, nor to the establishment of a dialogue between fate and contingency. The masks, within the rules of this game, denote a life that is freely invented, an existence in the process of elaborating and inventing itself. No law of society, morality or fate determines how these characters will accept or reject love, marriage, death or the ties of blood. Whence their apparent cynicism.

This theatre effects neither a catharsis nor a transposition of reality. It is at the same time a discovery and an invention. No basic questions are posed in advance. Its ethic is not dictated by a moral order, it is imposed by a lived reality, which is why this theatre never loses its freshness. Human relationships are not determined by codes, and even if such codes exist destiny is there with its improbabilities to show how fragile they are. Relationships are those of freedom. The actors do not have to pretend in order to get inside their roles. What they must do is enter into the game, assimilate in a total way the theatrical convention and invent their behaviour as they go along. It is not surprising that a great deal is left to improvisation.

With the Theatre of the Absurd, finally, the question of man's destiny becomes a questioning of theatre itself. The negation of theatre is a negation of the western form of relationship established between man and reality.

———————

The African Negro had no need of theatre or written stories. The jungle is not the desert, and the relationship with nature is instantaneously established and constantly renewed. The African identified himself with the forces of nature. He assimilated them by submitting to them. The celebration of nature became ritual. Nature was not deified in abstractions symbolizing the elements, nor was it a threat against which life must be defended. It was life itself, the eternal source. Its flood carries with it as many evils as blessings; its law must be accepted. Cannibalism is a part of this total attitude to nature. The strong man is the sorcerer who, thanks to invisible powers similar to those of nature, is able to bring order to anarchy and give coherence to a vitality that knows no law but that of its own exuberance. The African celebrates life through his alliance with and his submission to nature.

The discovery of the New World was to give a fresh start to the West. Where Europe had failed the virgin continent would perhaps succeed. But there is a price to be paid for being occidental. Every nation of Europe arrived on the new shores laden with all the attributes of the civilization that had grown up along the Mediterranean and the Atlantic. They left to conquer a new land, to conquer themselves and other men. In short, the European's quest for a relationship between man, nature, other men and himself went on as before.

What happened in North America? The Anglo-Saxons in the new world gave themselves the title of Pilgrims. They came to build on this unknown land a society that would mirror God's will and establish on earth the dominion and reign of the supreme power. How could they deal with a nature that was at once rich, exuberant and difficult? To admit of an alliance between man and nature would have been to proclaim a new vision of the relationship between man and himself. It would have been the spontaneous acceptance, without intermediary, of the forces of life. The marriage never took place, and nature was devastated. Of course it had to be conquered, but this conquest was at the same time a conquest of the self, a war against man's instincts and all the anarchic vital forces.

The native peoples were a part of the totality of life rejected by them. Natives had to be eliminated. The only good Indian, they said, was a dead one. Having devastated nature, they practiced genocide on its inhabitants and allies. The enslavement of this new domain available to man extended to the workers who had to be brought in to ensure the continued expansion of the Kingdom of God. Slavery is a direct consequence of a particular relationship between man and nature, between man and himself. Nature, devastated, took refuge (in the eyes of these new pilgrims) in the black man, the instinctual man, hypersexed, always ready to violate the immaculate white woman. To conquer the forces of nature and proclaim the Kingdom of God on earth one must also control one's own excesses. Work was not a means of earning a living and attaining happiness, it was a way to accomplish the work of God, the conquest of the exterior world and of the self. Everything that proclaims life in its primal anarchy is inspired by Satan. *The Crucible* illuminates man's fear of himself. Puritanism, by separating man from himself and alienating him from nature, gave him a margin of freedom never before attained in human history. The work of devastation and conquest bore fruit. Unparalleled material benefits made men fat without sating their hunger.

Some novelists tried to do in imagination what had not been done in reality. Huckleberry Finn finds in a dream-nature marvels about which his contemporaries could not and did not wish to know. But *Moby Dick* at the same time recounts the anguish of man who realizes that the Kingdom of God cannot be attained through the conquest of nature and the self, and that this struggle, in any case, is an endless one.

In the nineteen-fifties, when this civilization was approaching an impasse, new voices were heard: those of the blacks. Richard Wright, James Baldwin, Ralph Ellison, each in his own way, declared that the relationship of man to reality as it had developed in the United States was the bitter fruit of racism. Only the acceptance of life and oneself (assuming a solution to social and economic problems) could lead to genuinely human relations between blacks and whites.

22

Jewish writers, for their part, set about rediscovering America. Bernard Malamud and Saul Bellow proclaimed the primacy of life. They inspected all the myths on which the American psyche was built: innocence, the opening of the West, the maleficent forces of corruption. In *A New Life* Malamud makes his apologia for the everyday, but it is an everyday consecrated by birth, triumphant life and the dream. The victory he tries to achieve is a humble one. It is never complete. Bellow's *Herzog* is typical of the American who takes stock of all the stereotyped ideas and material blessings he enjoys, and concludes that in his feelings and his vital energy he is alienated; that he can no longer achieve a meeting of instinct and reality. This is an attempt to rediscover a direct relation between man and reality without the intermediary of the theatrical; but it is an abortive attempt, stopped at the level of desire or dream.

Then we encounter a new generation of writers who see this defeat and make it their task to invent a new kind of theatre. Bruce Jay Friedman, in *Stern* makes his official report: American man is fundamentally alienated. The only possible communication between Stern, the Jew, and his antisemitic Christian neighbour, is violence, an emancipating violence that prevents or at worst delays the descent into neurosis and madness.

Other writers are aware that dramatization must be inadequate, useless, in a world where man is estranged from himself. Despair is the keynote of their admission that theatre has failed. Novels by John Barth, Thomas Pynchon and Joseph Heller show us the grotesque face of drama turned upon itself and proclaiming, after a lucid look, its own impotence. Then there is the search for other paths of flight and escape: drugs, hallucination, the temptation of an artificial reality meant to replace the one which can no longer be rejoined. In Burroughs this lucid descent into Hell is a new kind of romanticism. The individual does not, as in the case of European romantics, project himself into an ideal or ethereal universe in order to counter a hated reality; he plunges into the dregs of his own inner world with no hope of attaining freedom, but rather with a desperate will to destroy himself.

This dramaturgy is not related (as tl   ɔf European romanticism was) to the projection of the adolescent as an autonomous individual seeking his place in an adult world. The American adolescent is also removed from the world of action and responsibility, but his attributes are more complex and ambiguous.

In America the accent is on youth. This is a way of prolonging the myth of innocence and that of the (as yet uncompleted) conquest of a virgin land. The age of reason is thus delayed, indefinitely postponed. People try to forget it. Youth itself becomes a myth and is reduced to a kind of theatre expressed in fashion, in music . . . Adults deprive adolescents of the only mediation left that might usher them into adulthood and give them some relationship to reality: that of their own youth. On the other hand these adolescents enjoy many adult privileges: they marry young, they start working young, they even have their own stars and heroes. They have all the components of a world apart, a universe for themselves, but their world leads to nothing, it is dispersed and frittered away before it can reach out to reality.

The American adolescent more than any other is in a state of total insecurity. His alienation is complete. Whence the search for new paths leading to reality. We see new forms of dramatization develop in this closed world of youth (closed, that is, to adults). Drugs of all kinds, bohemianism, political action. But these are flights from an unknown reality which has been rejected without trying to penetrate or change it. The deep crisis of American youth proceeds, then, from the absence of any link with reality, and from the periodic rise of kinds of dramatization that are abortive and ineffective, creating neither ritual nor social traditions capable of being handed down to a later generation.

24

At the same time we witness the birth of another kind of theatre, this time a reassuring one, which makes a cunning detour around the crisis. Its spokesman is Marshall McLuhan. When he proclaims that technology is no longer a simple channel of communication, he leads us to the conclusion that the dramaturgy born of the latest technical means (whether record, telephone or television) is no longer a mediator with reality but reality itself. When we say that the theatre is no longer an instrument of communication we abolish reality by confusing it with a theatre born of technology. Instead of facing the problems posed by the new relationships with reality which technical discoveries have made urgent, McLuhan eliminates these problems by eliminating reality itself. Reassuring indeed, but perhaps not for long.

A different kind of discovery of America was accomplished in Brazil. The first Portuguese who moored their ships on the shores of that new world did not come as pilgrims to set up the Kingdom of God on earth. Indeed, if they had attempted to do so nature would have raised formidable barriers against them. As it was, they wanted nothing more than to bask in life and luxury in this land where women were there for the taking and the excesses of nature corresponded to those of their own instincts. The Portuguese had neither the desire nor the energy to devastate such a profusely abundant land. They came as if to a fiesta. For generations the conquest of Brazil was also a triumph of eroticism. And when the Jesuits tried to impose some restraints on this anarchic marriage of man with nature, they could do no more than take note of the potency of this new relationship with reality. The only demand they could impose on the white man, who went his tireless way among the beds of white, black and Indian women, was that he recognize the fruits of his excesses. As long as his progeniture was baptized, the European way of life was secure. Brazil,

25

inheritor of Arab civilization via Portugal and bearer of Black Africa's culture, managed to retain the forms of Catholicism while creating the first New World civilization in which a direct rapport with reality was established, and in which the theatrical was not a mediator, not a refuge or an escape, but a ceremony, a celebration of the impulses of life perpetually renewed.

Eroticism permeates life in Brazil, but it is not a mechanized sexuality to be viewed with abhorrence. It is the expression of the acceptance of life. Brazil has had no race problem. It was inconceivable that a Brazilian, even of noble birth, might reject a woman because she was black. Marriages took place; and racism is non-existent in Brazil because the only race is one of mixed blood. Life is a fiesta. God's creation is one of happiness, of delights to be seized each day. Work is only a means of achieving this reward. Puritanism, of course, is at an opposite pole. If there are sexual barriers here, or frontiers which cannot be crossed, they are designed only to have a braking effect on the anarchy of this positive acceptance of life, not to act as symbols of its rejection. They are society's protection against its own overflowing vitality. But in this plunge into the flood of life there is also an indifference to the laws of material conquest. The efforts of this society are not as rigorously organized as in others where effort is a positive act of will rather than a sacrifice. Since there is no devastation of nature here (and in many regions of Brazil nature is severe and hostile), since work is not a matter of self-conquest, since reality is touched daily and there are no self-imposed restraints to lead to a neglect of reality, efficiency and the victories of materialism obviously are not at home in Brazil.

Submitting to other-worldly forces, the nomads who followed Mohammed from Mecca to Medina set out to conquer the world. This was their way of affirming man's victory over nature, which, once subdued, assured them of earthly happiness. The travels of the faithful of Islam are very different from those that led Abraham from Ur in Chaldea to the Promised Land. His alliance with God, which ensured a complicity with nature and gave to life a resultant unity, is not repeated in Islam. History is the domain of the Moslems. To triumph over time they subjected themselves to the notion of duration and, by obeying its laws, became its masters. Reality was not, for them, some intemporal nature, a life of perpetual rebirth, a project never finished because it belonged to all time; it was, rather, the accomplishment of the desires of a higher will, within a particular framework: that of *history*.

For the Jews the Garden of Eden existed before the birth of time. In the Koran, Paradise exists in another world and is a reward for those who have accomplished God's will in history. As described in the Koran it is a place where nature flourishes without restraint, its forces totally subject to man's desires. The Promised Land has been transplanted to heaven.

The theatrical is not abolished in Islam: its stage is history. Man's relationship to reality is mediated by the temporal act of satisfying a higher will. Time becomes the great mediator. It is the theatre in which man and reality are brought face to face. The emigration, the hegira, is the beginning of a triumphal march: man married to time and its passage. A new era begins. But the obstacles turn out to be insurmountable. Opposing forces prevent history from taking the desired course. And man himself gives in to his own nature; he cannot wait to pluck the fruits of Paradise in the next world, as promised. He wants them now, in green lands that will make him forget the rigours of the desert. The nomad settles down, builds the Alhambra, and relaxes into decadence. In the end, history triumphs over Islam. The Ottoman conquerors take up the march, yet their main goal is not to bring about a meeting of man with reality. It is

27

conquest for its own sake. The Ottoman parenthesis remains marginal in the great adventure of Islam.

For centuries the Arabs interiorized history. Turning to their own past was not, for the Arab nationalists at the beginning of this century, the result of their nostalgia for lost grandeurs of other centuries, but of their desire to re-establish contact with reality by re-entering the stream of history.

But medieval Europe had meanwhile become the seat of industrial and colonial powers. Islam had no strength with which to oppose it. There were many moves, escapist or imitative, to set up a revived Orient against the West. We still see Islam served up in fascist, communist or socialist sauces, and there have been innumerable attempts to prove that secular religion is not incompatible with the industrial era. But the great misfortune of the Arab countries is that they have still not succeeded in reinserting themselves in history, which more and more reveals itself as theatre. The past becomes a refuge, a consolation and a stimulant. A people that extended its empire from China to Spain has proven itself. But this dramatization founders on a reality that turns the old triumph into a trivial anachronism. Yet the dramatization persists, and festers. The Arabs' will to self-realization in history, in spite of history, cannot, must not be reduced to a hollow dream prompted by vanity. It is the will to re-establish the relationship with reality to which nomads aspire when they leave the desert. One does not change the kind of relationship one has established with reality, especially if it has been a fruitful one. For the western mind, the frenzied insistence of Arabs on recapturing their place in history appears as a childish contempt for reality. But the Arabs can adopt the western mode of mediation with reality only if they themselves undergo a fundamental change. Levantinism is the proof that one cannot with impunity adopt an Occident composed of objects and appearances.

28

The Arab Orient is going through the anguish of its inadaptability to the present world. It can no longer afford to relive the dramatization of its past history in a mood of nostalgia and passive expectation. But neither can it re-insert this dramatization into the present. History is slipping away from it, but it cannot resign itself to abandoning all control over its own history, for this would mean that the relationship it has established with reality is false, not in the temporary sense that applied for some centuries of foreign conquest and occupation, but more fundamentally: because the Orient, master again of its own armies and governments, can no longer bring its relationship to reality into harmony with its re-involvement in history.

The techniques of the industrial age are not a closed book to the Arabs. But these techniques cloud their relationship with reality. They cannot industrialize the Orient without adapting technology to the particular relationship the Arab Orient has established with reality. If the Orient is not to disappear as a mode of humanity and a vision of the world, new relations between technology and man must be invented. The Arab elites have not shown themselves dynamic enough to accept the challenge. The Moslem Brotherhood represents a last-ditch rejection of the West, while Communism and Nazism are, in this context, used in an attempt to turn western ideologies against the West itself. In the final analysis, there is no proof that history can again become the mediator between the Arab and reality.

All Arabs, as individuals, have known for generations that if history escapes their grasp it is because of their defective relationship with reality. Collectively, they affirm their will to connect with their past (that is, to re-establish their rapport with reality) in a kind of feast which is at the same time a celebration and a demonstrative waiting. This is why their political manifestations are as violent as they are sporadic. The need lies close to the surface in the life of each individual, and a spark can set off a manifestation of the collective will. Such dramatizations are reminiscent of those which gave Arab history its substance, but they are not even shadows of the earlier ones. They leave no mark on history, find no place in time.

Insertion in history has never entirely satisfied the Arab's desire to establish a relationship with reality. We can see this in the period during which history seemed totally submissive to the will of the Islamic faithful. In order to enjoy completely and personally the conquests accomplished by their caliphs and heroes, the subjects of Haroun al Rashid invented legends that set a distance between man and history, so that the grandeur of events should not end by engulfing man or effacing the last trace of his individuality. *The Thousand and One Nights* provided a safety valve for men who were not satisfied to live their history, however heroic it might be. But the elite, the leaders, were forced to reject this dramaturgy which answered only the needs of those who, unable to insert themselves into history, turned it into legend.

But the individual Arab has another choice. After the collective interiorization of the drama of history, he interiorized his personal theatre. His relations with reality and with other men are established spontaneously, immediately. No abstraction dictates his line of conduct. He is sincere in the sense that his relationships are spontaneous. But his sincerities can vary throughout a series. The Westerner, used to an oblique relationship with reality and to the mediation of abstractions, is too prone to accuse the Arab of hypocrisy. He has encountered not two-facedness but two spontaneous and successive reactions. Human relations among Arabs border upon play, but the game is known and accepted by both parties. The protagonists fall back on this theatricality because a direct rapport with reality escapes them. There remain, to be sure, certain collective virtues which are still effective, dating from the days when Arabs were for the most part nomadic. Politeness, honour, hospitality, pride, generosity – these were the themes of pre-Islamic poetry,

30

and persist as the qualities that give substance to the individual in our time.

What accentuates the inadaptation of Arabs to the modern world is the hiatus separating the personal and collective dramatizations of each individual. Thus their dickering, which in the bazaars is a limited personal theatre, a dramatic game whose spectators are also the actors, may also prove effective on the larger stage of world politics; but its effectiveness is bound to be ephemeral. By the same token, if there is a connection between words and reality, and if words are often an escape from the constraints of reality, words acquire the virtue of duration when pronounced by heads of state before a world-wide public.

The violence we see in the Orient is that of a human community which cannot forget its character, and which is unable to preserve that character if it acquires again its former prominence in history. And because the dramatization is lived collectively and individually every day, appearances are as important as that which they conceal. The function of the mask is not to expose reality to the light of day; it represents another facet of that reality. Whence the importance of saving face. To make a show of strength or generosity is as important as really being strong or generous. The same applies to friendship. It is not enough to declare a sincere and durable feeling for someone, continual proofs must be given in word and act. This kind of theatre, foreign to the western mind, is a source of inconvenience to the Oriental, for it isolates him from the modern world and the technology to which he aspires and feels attracted.

––––––––––––

Europe, slaughtering its Jews, tried to smother its dream of a primal Orient. The relationships that the West has established with reality are in extremely delicate equilibrium. The irrational forces of nature and instinct erupt occasionally to remind the masters of technology that control of nature is

31

still beyond their grasp. The mediation of abstractions has not led to a victory for man. Psychoanalysis has, in fact, revealed the abyss of nihilism within. Nazism channelled the irrational, and made a weapon of it. Nazism, to succeed, had to eliminate all memory of a harmonious and immediate relationship between man and reality. The irrational was dramatized, and the dramatization had as its goal the subjection of man. Nazism is the triumph of nature, the negation of the other world and of man himself.

German romanticism was the expression of a profound malaise. It was in Germany that dramatization reached the extreme limit of abstraction. It was here that music, beginning with Bach, gave to the emotional life of the West a geometry that screened it from reality. But even the transparency of concept and melody do not free man from the contingencies of life. The event is always there to call him to order. Whence the temptation of Faust, and the Nietzschian explosion, both trying to impose man's will on reality. Such attempts to establish a relationship with reality through an affirmation of man's strength spring from an exaggerated vision of his powers.

It is not surprising that Germany was the scene of the most strenuous effort, not only to reject the presence of the Jew as witness to the persistance of a primal Orient, but to exterminate him. It is also not astonishing to find, among the torturers in the concentration camps, men who are brought to tears by the sound of music. In the universe of dramatization, when theatre has lost all contact with reality and fulfils no mediating function, men can only pass from one abstraction to another.

––––––––––––––––

The survivors of the holocaust have not forgotten the ancient dream of Judaism. To return to the Orient is to admit the failure of Jewish penetration of the West. But how did this return come about?

The idea of a national state which would reassemble dispersed and persecuted Jews had its birth in a Europe where nationalism had taken on a double task: to channel individual romanticisms into collective action; and at the same time make of the abstraction "Nation" a new mediator between man and reality — a liturgy to replace the relationship with the beyond. If we add to this nationalism the hopes for an egalitarian and socialist society, we can understand the attraction these ideas had for Jews anxious at the same time to play their part in a modernist renewal of life and to conserve what was unique in their own culture. So from the start the national Jewish state was an ancestral land and the place where a new relationship between man and nature was to be achieved. Without waiting for the age of the Messiah the pioneers hoped to accomplish the ancient dream of Judaism, not as marginal pockets in hostile societies but in their own right, in accordance with the dream itself.

But the twentieth century inexorably exacted its price. To build a state it is necessary to plunge into a reality one has not chosen: the colonizing power has hostile neighbours. The holocaust gave a new direction to the millenial dream. Before life can acquire its quality and savour it must be made safe, and there is only one way to do this. Refugees must be fed and lodged, and their right to stay must be defended by force of arms. And so a state is built after well-tried models. The West, which for centuries has forced the Jews to lead a restricted life, seems, in this rediscovered Orient, to be a goal and an ideal. Voices are raised to affirm that Israel is a western country, an extension of Europe. Nothing could be more natural at a time when the success of western technology is undisputed, especially among the large number of socialists and *bundists* who came not to revive Judaism but to help Jews achieve a European humanism (which, in its place of birth, had ended if not in failure at least in an impasse).

And so we see a skeletal Orient, materially and spiritually exhausted, sharing the Promised Land with

33

Europeans who refuse to leave Europe behind. They proclaim that the oriental Jew has only one path to follow: that of the West. The oriental Jews, ignorant of their heritage and their own character, ask nothing better than to enjoy the comforts of technological progress. They assume a western style and despise as out-of-date the relics of their past. Yet whether they like it or not, they are condemned to constituting a resistance movement. Even if they adopt a reassuring Levantinism, their real allies are the land where they live, and the quest for man of which Judaism has been the highest and most tragic expression. They will, no doubt, be sacrificed, and will themselves be the first to bury an aspiration that appears more and more antiquated and, above all, impractical.

A third group remains to be mentioned: those who dream of a living absolute. The liberals and liberated cannot reject the bearded ones of Mea Chearim without feeling a certain unease. Yet from the point of view of builders of a modern state, western and efficient, these are fanatics who are incapable of resigning themselves to an acceptance of reality. Defiantly, these few men on the margin of society have set themselves up as guardians of an absolute. Yet the order they dream of establishing is not a mystical one. It aspires to a way of life in which the alliance of man with God is brought about without dramaturgy, and in which the relationship with reality is reached without recourse to any mediation. But the more this vision of the world is driven into a marginal position, the more the way of life becomes an absolute. What is universal takes on the appearance of a splinter sectarianism, and the quest for the concrete is transmuted into dreams. The resistance of these "guardians" to what seems to them a treasonable perversion is not without its own ambiguities and confusions. Their behaviour bears the marks of a long association with the Christian mystics and theologians of Kiev, Odessa and Cracow. Yet the memory of original Judaism is what makes these incorrigibles move and live, even as their will to live according to that

34

Judaism turns to exacerbation and violence, because they can barely survive among men who want to forget what *they* remember, who want no more than the comfort to be found in the anonymity of the western world.

————————————

The theatre which has played a great role in the material success of the West may lead to a question-mark, or to alienation, or the absurd; but the attempt of the Orient to do without the mediation of a dramaturgy also ends in failure because it cannot construct a material civilization without making use of western norms. The desire for a direct relationship with reality does not die but is diverted along the ways of art and literature.

There is no paradox in saying that the actor is the one who draws the dividing line between theatre and direct contact with reality. He takes part in western civilization, and though dramatization penetrates the daily life of western man, the latter notices the fact only in moments of crisis when, in despair and anger, he becomes aware of his basic alienation.

The actor lives his dramatization consciously. He knows that a relationship with theatre is problematical, risky and necessary. He chooses to be a man divided, and it is thus that he finds his own unity. The theatre for him is not an escape, it is a consciously adopted mediation. The actor is western man pushed to the extreme. His equilibrium is real, even if he achieves it at the price of a constant tension. To be an actor is to make a conscious choice to be occidental. The delicacy of such an equilibrium is palpable. If the actor succeeds in establishing a relationship with reality, it is thanks to the public. He knows that he is alive because he succeeds, through a division of his own being, in moving, captivating and swaying a crowd. For him the spectator is reality — though not, of course, the whole of reality. The actor has his intimate, personal side which he manages to keep more or less intact. He can be no more than a symbol because reality becomes a spectacle only at certain moments, often privileged moments. Artists, novelists, poets and painters have always tried to capture these privileged moments, to make of them an instrument of communication with reality for a public limited in neither time nor space.

There are no easy solutions, no ready-made recipes. The possibilities are as varied as the problems. Pirandello's plays are about the theatre itself. In Beckett nothing remains but words, themselves the expression of ultimate despair. The *nouveau roman* is undoubtedly the last resort of an Occident which is at a complete impasse. But it is also the expression of a need for some new discovery of reality. Even if reality exists only through words which hint at its presence in the abyss, these words at least are listing objects and gestures in order to make a kind of balance-sheet of whatever reality may exist behind abstractions and affective interpretations. To be sure, this ersatz reality will end up as a party game, for if it exists independently of man he cannot integrate it or make it coincide with reality.

Some American novelists have tried more modest solutions. Their rediscovery of reality is not limited to words. Bellow and Malamud among others try to make contact between the objects around them, the traditions that nourish them and the impulses of the heart. Malamud as much as says, finally, that the Jew he describes is a universal character, and that in fact all men are Jews, to the extent that they are also artists.

In France poets have explored avenues where novelists seldom venture. Mallarmé, and after him Valéry, tried to make the subject of poetry poetry itself, to transform the abstract concept into a secondary reality that could satisfy both mind and heart. Nearer to our own time, Guillevic and Ponge are namers of objects. They are discovering in words certain virtues that have been familiar to Jews and Arabs for centuries. Grosjean goes farther in this direction and draws

36

directly from oriental sources. But the concept, second nature to the West, crops up again in Guillevic in the form of geometric figures. Bonnefoy has chosen the most difficult path, not turning his back on the concept but integrating it into a reality that he creates piece by piece, a reality that is not ersatz. Rather than fleeing to a fictitious Orient, he tries, by returning to the great tradition of the West, to make of a secular civilization a reality that one can cling to, though not through the concept, for the concept is overtaken by the material phenomena it has created. Bonnefoy knows that the innocence of the Orient cannot be recaptured. But theatre too must end in its own negation, and the West is reborn through its own death.

The attempts of poets or novelists, however, are no more than a kind of nostalgia or remembrance. The relationship to reality is still no more than a desire. The artist is the first to know that in the privileged moments when man spontaneously establishes his relationship to reality – and it is given to men to know love, to attain privileged moments which the artist does no more than capture and arrest – he often chooses to describe what he cannot attain or perpetuate, knowing that what he does is no more than a testimony to expectations, the avowal of a sense of loss. But he has only one other choice: self-forgetfulness. If that is his choice, man's desire to establish contact with reality (in other words, to live) is swallowed up in silence.

The Image and the Unseen

It was the immoderation of the cathedral of Notre Dame that struck me, its absurdity. I did not presume to think of its lack of utility, for I admired the West too much. This place of prayer could not make me forget the synagogue that stood back-to-back with the house where I was born. My father used to take me there as if it had been a café. We felt at home, we were among neighbours. Children who lived nearby ran through the aisles between the benches. Solemnity was reserved for the biblical Word; what we read then was a timeless language. On the Sabbath and feast days there was song, suddenly filled with meaning. It was in His own language that we addressed the Master of the universe. And the familiarity of our call to Him was in accord with the intimacy of the place itself.

As a child I used to walk past the mosques, much impressed by their minarets. I did not dare go inside. The very idea of violating a sacred place filled me with terror. And yet the doors were wide open and nothing prevented me from crossing the threshold. What stopped me was the awareness that I was confronted by a strange world that was not my own. Later it was the rich ornamentation and the majesty of the decor that made these places of meeting and prayer inaccessible to me. And yet when, at the age for growing a little defiant of religion, I went in with Moslem friends, the interior seemed to me even poorer and more ascetic than that of the synagogue in my quarter of the city. There were not even benches in this vast, naked hall.

To see Notre Dame in its full dimensions one had to back away from it. These towers rising to infinity, these walls, crushing in their majesty, commanded admiration and respect. It was not a house with its back to my house, with a song rising within. It was a monument. In a confused way I realized that art was born in Europe and that it had a precise meaning. The cathedral is no more than the symbol, the eloquent incarnation of a specific order, a relationship established by man with God, a relationship with nature.

Mohammed's first act was to break the statues of Kuraych. Islam in the Kaaba venerates a stone of abstract form. Thus nature is reduced to a faceless symbol. The reign of God is total. Man has a direct relationship with Him. The sole mediator is the word, and it is already God's. Nature is no more than a place where man carves out his existence while affirming the reign of God. Nature is the enemy, for the man of the deserts knows that it is the bringer of death, and that his only protection is his alliance with God. What could be the point of ingratiating oneself with blind Nature by paying homage to the symbols of its power? It must be reduced to a stone.

And when the Jews, as they waited for the Promised Land, set up in the nakedness of the desert a golden calf whose richness contrasted with and made them forget their own deprivation, they were punished for it. Between God and man no statue can be interposed without nature becoming a mediator or refuge.

At the moment when man first inscribed his own image in stone he succumbed to the temptation to pay nature a kind of homage which in fact prefigured an abdication, a first step towards acceptance of defeat. To leave a trace, inscribe a visible design, raise up an image of oneself — these are attempts to perpetuate oneself in the immutability of stone. Man thereby accepts the fact that his own construction survives him. In the alliance between the movement which ends in death, and the immobility that is the sovereign quality of stone, he seeks a refuge in which to hide from the beyond and affirm his own autonomous presence. And as if he feels that his attempt is doomed to failure he tries to liberate God from the limitations of the word; the divine presence is inscribed in stone, assumes a face, becomes an image. God is confined to a building erected by man, to whom he delegates his power. God is no longer a face (shekhina), no longer a word, but a person who consecrates stone by sanctifying it, and perpetuates man's power by making him master of everyday destinies. Interceding powers rise up from the shadows. God has representatives, God has vicars. And as if this extremity of pride, this madness had extended its empty effrontery to man's most vain pretensions, he accepts the laws of his own defeat. It is not life that is inscribed on his stones, but the loss of life. Man perpetuated in nature is man crucified, and his vicars accept sterility. They do not pass life along. Thus the separation becomes complete. From the marriage of movement and immobility is born a man who dies. True life is elsewhere. The breath of God can reanimate only in the next world.

These soaring naves are meant to bring men closer to a God hidden behind clouds; they are built by men who worship Him and seek in collective ceremony to create a dwelling that will outlast them. Each time I went into a church I was struck by this spontaneous decision to set in stone man's testimony to a splendour he liked to think was potentially visible. On my first visit to Versailles I tried to imagine the palace of Haroun al Rashid. The caliphs came and went, and left but one name in the great book of history. But here the memory of the pettiest French lord persists in walls that have defied the years. The cathedral inscribes in stone the relationship between man and God, and attests to the sovereignty of man in an unchanging nature. The Prince raises up his palace as an affirmation of a relationship between men which consecrates the master's power in a world in which stone is sovereign. The lord is not chief of a tribe that roams the desert, challenging hostile nature with his wisdom and courage, but a master whose power is expressed in the green acreage he occupies. Yet it was in Europe that I saw a true Arab palace, the Alhambra. Here I saw nature vanquished, put at man's service, not as a mediator with the beyond, nor a stage on the road to the absolute. The gardens are arranged to give shade and freshness. And what refinements are devoted to ensuring the ease of the body in the bath halls!

For centuries the West constructed buildings and painted images not to remind themselves of the existence of a beyond but to confine it within the abode of man. The colour of God was there for the eye, his silhouette for every gaze. In this subtle, skilful and despairing game, man, in full flower but troubled, talked to himself in the firm belief that he was talking to God. A whole civilization was built on this desire to create a link between the sovereignty of God and the power of man. How could the latter come closer to God than by imitating Him? And so, far from attaining the kingdom of heaven, he transformed it into a theatre. He had recourse to spectacle as a substitute for direct contact with God. For centuries the West believed in the power of art, the frenzied attempts to approach God by celebrating the image, an attempt which quickly transformed itself into the dream of stealing a piece of God's power by imitating his act of creation. Now the image leaves the church walls and becomes autonomous. Out of nothingness the painter evokes his testimony to the sovereignty of man become creator in his turn. But the painter is merely a creator of images.

Protestantism was the revolt of men who, too close to a nature that reigned through mythology, despaired of attaining God through the intercession of theatre. In fact, their return to sources, their Bible-reading in the original language, their churches purged of graven images, were a negation not of Catholic theatre but of the element of oriental sensuality which (at times and to a degree) deflected the theatrical away from its vain aspirations to divinity and toward a celebration of human joy and earthly happiness. There is a great gap between the bleeding Christ of the German painters and the smiling, almost happy Christ of the Italian medieval schools. It was not the lushness of the Orient

41

that Luther's followers sought in the Hebraic Bible, but rather the authority of an immutable foreign scripture that could be interpreted as coinciding with their will to redirect earthly existence along the paths of guilt and redemption. The Vicars of Christ were not eliminated so that life might triumph, but in order that the sign of death should become indelible.

No painter has had such an effect on me as Rembrandt. On each visit to Holland I found new sources of wonder. He never ceased painting his own portrait, because he would not accept, would not recognize that the power of art is derisory. He knew that a portrait once fixed on the canvas is transformed into a mask in the absence of the breath of Life. This is a man who saw the idol in closeup, who understood that the Orient could not, without denying its relationship with God, allow the idol to exist. Rembrandt knew that the tragic could not be the theme of a painting without being dissipated in the theatrical. (Think of the multitude of masks by Franz Hals!) It was because Rembrandt mistrusted the face, and saw the threat in it, that he made every feature transparent, erasing it as it took form on his canvas, trying to make it opaque. He lived too close to the Orient, too close to Jewry, for his paintings of the ghetto world not to sparkle with an immediate joy, a joy without reticence to which he was a passive witness. To go on believing in the power of painting would have led him to lose his faith in the power of God. He ceded to the evidence, celebrating in his works the power of God, that of the Bible. And this was not, in fact, a defeat. In putting his painting at the service of God he was trying to provide it with a *raison d'être* – not an attempt calculated to give him peace of mind. He knew that he would always live on the margin of reality, that the Orient (so near in that Amsterdam ghetto where one could lose oneself, find oneself) became no more than theatre for one who remained on its threshold or wished only to be a spectator. Rembrandt surrendered to a faith that he no longer tried to reconcile with art, because a relationship with the beyond is not within the scope or power of art. Art could only be subordinated to a quest of a different order. This recognition of the existence of a boundary between the spheres of art and faith makes the artist's quest appear, not merely inadequate and ineffective, but totally useless and futile.

In the case of Jordaens, painting is no longer mediation but compensation. This convert to Calvinism initiates the excesses of Puritan art. Men and women are shown in a delirium of gluttony and drunkenness. Their obesity is not a sign of sensual joy, but of their avidity to compensate for their refusal of life. Vermeer consciously accepted that painting should be theatrical. His paintings are composed like backdrops. For him painting has lost its power of mediation. The theatre he elaborates has an accepted everyday setting. He attempted to equate life, something given and immediate, with a happiness which did not open onto the beyond, could not escape into the imagination. What is transfigured is daily life, and art is no more than a struggle against time, a refusal of its consequences. But if daily life is not sanctified, it is reduced to spectacle. Many generations were satisfied by this daily life, its monotony enlivened and interrupted by political and commercial adventures. From this time on, the paths of redemption were those of work and conquest. Finally this apparent tranquility, this acceptance of forgetfulness, were carried to the point of madness. Van Gogh would accept neither defeat nor resignation. If the power of art was limited, if it could not act as mediator in a relationship with God, the whole scaffolding of the West collapsed, condemned from the start. Could God be unattainable and the world an accident devoid of meaning? What if art were no more than the decor of an illusory world, a futile dream of creation in the void? In this event art becomes a theatre of madness, an admission of the absence of God.

In France Delacroix accepted that painting should be theatrical, on condition that it not be reduced to a simple decor but tell a story: one in which man reassured himself that his passing was not an affair of chance but something with a beginning and an end, something that endured within time. In the Orient he sought out images, if not proofs, illustrating harmony with the world and a sensual relationship with nature and between men. At the very moment of western triumph this primal Orient was a reminder that theatrical mediation ends by being self-sufficient, and cannot approach a relationship with reality.

The consequences were predictable. Matisse accepted only the decorative aspects of the Orient. He made of painting a decor as sensual as one could wish, flattering the eye with its richness but incapable of surviving the moment. His return to the Orient is a defeat accepted and recognized as such. His Orient was one that could never touch me. It seemed to me to be an improper takeover, exploitation in a low key.

More disquieting was the approach of Bonnard. I remember the retrospective of 1947, which was the first big exhibition of paintings I had ever visited. Behind apparently harmonious colours, behind calm lines without the shade of a tremor, confusedly I felt the anguish of an era's termination. I know now that Bonnard had realized that the powers of art were suited neither to creating a bridge between man and reality nor to consoling him for its absence. In Bonnard I find an expression of man's solitude in space, a solitude made no less acute by his mastery of the elements. For centuries art had served as a mediator, yet the relationship with God was just as elusive. But if painting survives despite its inefficacy as a mediator, if it persists beyond its defeat, it is because it has some meaning. Namely, it questions its own meaning.

Henceforth art has its place not outside the world but in it, with no need or wish to justify or explain it. We return to the first forms of Oriental decoration. Yet between those arabesques and calligraphic decorations and the forms of abstract art there is a basic difference. The Semitic East had never allowed figurative art, not only because it felt no need for it, but also because it seemed obvious that any mediating art prevented and corrupted the relationship between man

44

and reality. By forbidding all human images in paint or stone Judaism and Islam confirmed an order of things that pre-dated them: any theatrical relationship between man and reality would make inoperative the bond between man and God as conceived by Judaism and Islam. As a consequence art can be no more than a decor, an embellishment. It heightens the powers of sensuality. It is the celebration of a life that welcomes the real without mediation. And when Islam absorbed other civilizations with great pictorial traditions – India, Indonesia and Persia – it neutralized their art without abolishing it, by reducing it to decoration, to the embellishment of the word of the Koran. One needs only to visit the Museum of *Jewish Art* in New York in order to realize that the very terms are contradictory.

Western art cannot deny its past. Still less can it ignore the western version of the relationship between man and reality. But this art has turned into an interrogation of that relationship. Is art too ineffective to fulfill its mediating function? Or does the flaw lie in a system that calls for an art which mediates?

From being an interrogation of itself, painting passes into interrogation of the world. Picasso reversed the question posed by Bonnard. What tantalized him was not the power of art, but the power of the world to express itself and exteriorize itself through art, to last beyond the spontaneity of the moment or the recorded memory of the event. For him art is simply an instrument for the exploration of the real. And in this sense one can say that Picasso is not a painter and perhaps not even an artist. His approach is eminently religious. He is looking for the secret order of the world, for the harmony between the appearance of life on earth and the indifference of nature: a harmony that the Orient had stipulated without being able to live it out. He tries to attain, through this art for which he has no respect, a balance between man and things which would make his art irrelevant, incongruous and pointless.

45

Braque, on the other hand, tried continually to test the power of painting in order to understand the rapport of man with reality.

The experiments of modern painting have their starting point in objectives of a private nature. It may attempt to be efficient, utilitarian, astonishing, disturbing, exotic, ephemeral or decorative, but it has no reference point in a total notion of man, except in cases where anguish shows its face unveiled: in Giacometti, for example.

If we refuse the notion that art has a function of intercession, it becomes an accessory of the body and the place, lasting only as long as it remains useful. In these conditions it is difficult to attribute autonomy to art.

———————————————

In Arabic or Hebrew, when a word names an object it denotes an immediate harmony between the world and man's expression of it. Because this direct harmony between man and reality is absent in the West, the word acquires an existence of its own. It is an abstraction which plays its role in the elaboration of the theatrical. Western poetry tries to find its way back to the innocence of the word, to its rebirth, leading to a new identification with the object. When the word ceases to be an incantation celebrating a place nearby but invisible, present but intangible, when it ceases to be the material of which the theatre is built, it ceases to be a mediator between man and reality. It becomes an inquiry into its own nature. As the painter no longer believes in the power of the image, the western poet begins to question the power of the word. And the theatre begins its own self-examination. Thus, everything in the West which previously served as a mediator between man and the beyond, everything that served to establish a relationship between man and reality, turns in upon itself. Art, grown autonomous, feeds on itself, and perpetuates itself without reference to the world. It is as if man, accepting his own absence from the world and admitting the unbridged gulf between himself and God, were to invest art with a sovereignty which, while creating autonomy for art, proved its actual vanity and uselessness. The distance between man and the world grows wider with every material achievement. The West is on a perilous path where alienation from God is accompanied by alienation from one's neighbour. At the apogee of his material success western man finds himself imprisoned in an impenetrable solitude.

Protestantism was the first rejection of occidental theatre as developed by Christianity. Nature was no longer the only source from which man could obtain his living and affirm his place in the visible world. As cities and commerce grew, the occupation of land was no longer the only condition for survival. Theatre had to be given a new impetus, it had to be freed from decor and territoriality, and work had to become something more than a material necessity. It became a new form of mediation, the testimony to a relationship with God. Prayer was no longer confined to the interior of the church. In trying to liberate Christianity from its theatrical mode of expression the theatre was enlarged to include the whole world. Protestantism's perception of the weakness of religious dramaturgy in new social conditions led only to the need for a different dramaturgy. The new one had pretensions of being a return to a direct relationship with reality through a rediscovery of sources, but in reality it was a reaffirmation of the old dramaturgy in a form that freed it of elements that had hampered its effectiveness.

The new dramaturgies of nationalism and, later, Marxism, had no intention of establishing a link with the beyond. The community of man was self-sufficient, and its abstract self-portrait was a replacement for God. A relationship with God came to be seen as an obstacle to the creation of the fraternal community of men. This is the same slope on which the artist lost his footing. He ended by losing his belief in art as mediator, at the same time realizing that the world he created could be self-sufficient. But if that created world did not relate to reality it became a game, a mere diversion.

At the moment when France was proclaiming the triumph of its universality, and this theatrical vision of itself was proving its effectiveness as an instrument of conquest, Mallarmé encountered the impasse from which western literature still has found no exit. If an equivalence between word and object becomes impossible, the word is no longer a valid tool of communication. Each word is afflicted with duplicity, and the poet attempts to give it a new life. The difficulty lies more in the impossibility of direct communication than in the ambiguity of meaning. As the poet purifies language and searches for its original vigour, he does no more than elaborate a new dramaturgy. The poem is no longer an expression of reality, nor a link with a reality that has been rediscovered. It is a mediation with a reality that has vanished and can never be revived. It is ineffective. What is more, it nurtures and thus accentuates the overweening aspirations of dramaturgy. This is a dramaturgy with no object: for if the real is not only masked but inaccessible and if God no longer permeates the world, poetry becomes no more than a cry which, at best, can take the form of song and consolation.

Mallarmé's blank page is not an expression of temporary discouragement, nor even of a surrender to the temptation to pause and rest. It is a bleak gaze upon the basic impotence of all literary expression.

Baudelaire's cry was that of desolate man left to his own devices. In the outer landscape, natural and human, he sought a relationship with a world God had abandoned. Rimbaud defied this absent God with imprecations, frenzy and exasperation. He attempted to create a world in the image of Rimbaud. Not a refuge nor a haven of forgetfulness, not an imaginary place where he could flee from the world's ugliness, but an invented reality, created as a counterpart of the given world which had been imposed upon him. For him to succeed, the word would have had to have the power of reality, to be not an instrument, link or plaything but a true life attained directly by the poet, without mediation. Here western pride verges on madness. This is its hour of pathetic grandeur. It senses the limitations of the power of the word; it is doomed to failure. It reaches the peak of its triumph at the moment when it begins to decipher the augurs of its defeat. The Orient can give neither help nor consolation. This is the carrion place where Europe's pride has its fall, where western man, born of a civilization that clutched at life (while gazing, fascinated, at death) comes to meet his humiliating end. Pride that refuses to cede to resignation spends its final energy losing itself in the crowd. Loti, Flaubert, even Chateaubriand, who turned to the Orient for reassurance, seeking in it their own faith in universality (a justification rather than a questioning of the West), were obliged to invent an Orient that did not exist. Rimbaud was too lucid or too young to accept such a lie, such a glaring piece of obfuscation.

It was in Ireland that the exploration of language, of literary expression as a mediation with reality, was to reach its logical conclusion. Joyce could have been the product of no other land than this — one that embraced Catholicism without making theatre of it. Centuries of refusal of the Anglo-Saxon West, of the British variety of theatre, of the individual raised to the level of myth, ended in exasperation. In the name of what particularism could one resist a triumphant empire which offered equality as the reward for Irish resignation and abandonment of self? The dilemma of Ireland, this periphery of the western world, was its inability to lay claim to its own relationship with reality while refusing that which was imposed upon it. A particularism had to be invented, built from nothing. Joyce realized perfectly that

49

Irish nationalism was no more than a shrunken version of English nationalism. He saw his countrymen, in their quest for a different kind of relationship with reality, fall back on the notion they had of themselves, wrap themselves in a myth that hindered every movement, every innovation; he saw them use defiance and protest not to liberate unused sources of life, but to commit themselves to a slow death.

Unlike the Jews, the Irish could not turn to a primal Orient. They gained possession of their territory; but their religion, far from protecting their uniqueness, obliged them — supreme misunderstanding — to recognize themselves in the universal dogmas of Rome. Their final distinction was a language which no one in this day and age wanted to speak, much less write, and their defiance of the West was limited to their attempt to revive this dead language. Betrayed in their relationship with nature, abandoned by a God with whom they had the summary bond of a theatre imposed from outside, they could establish a relationship with their fellows only by preserving the image they had of themselves, by inventing their own particularism. And in this search for a direct relationship with reality, their return to a mother tongue seemed like a rediscovery of harmony with self, like a victory over the division in one's being. But what, in fact, is a language? Is it a simple instrument, a neutral mechanism without emotive implications, or a tool that becomes a cumbersome myth when certain virtues and powers are improperly attributed to it? And if the word is no more than a mirror of the object, what is the use of literature? Is it a simple chronicle in which man tries to survive through the traces he leaves in memory?

Since its beginnings the Orient has lived with this problem and has denied the word all powers save those of setting down the chronicle and communicating the reasoning and passions of men. The moment the word ceased to be a tool it became sacred. When it became song, or a prayer addressed to God, man himself became the instrument; the word was pronounced by God and man was its channel. Of

50

course, words served not only as tools of individual or collective communication on the one hand or of prayer on the other. At the height of Islam, Arab poets were aware that the word can serve to build an autonomous world, a dramaturgy to console man and make him forget an unattainable reality, even when it is unsuccessful in creating a bridge between man and that reality. In Islam the bridging was incomplete. In Islam's heroic age all writing that was not clandestine was obliged to go masked. All profane poetry was attributed to the pre-Islamic era, Al Jahiliya, the age of ignorance when man's eyes were still sealed to the truth.

The West endowed the word with power to replace reality, to be reality. If one could speak to God by the mediation of his vicars, if God was present through the image, his word was no longer a message of which man was at once receiver and transmitter, but life, reality. Literature, this world created by men, became not just a bridge to reality but reality itself. Rimbaud reacted with revolt and fury to the folly of this pretension. Joyce tried to put it to the test. He accepted exile to the periphery so that from this distance he could judge the dramaturgy by which the West lived. Because reality was fading into forgetfulness men were content to inhabit a second-hand world, an ersatz world.

Were there still forces that resisted the invasion of the ersatz? Yes, life at its most violent and naked: eroticism – a drive that the West had not succeeded in weakening. Thus the main character in Joyce is a Jew who attempts through the pursuit of the erotic to attain or re-attain life. But the erotic eludes him. Apart from his dreams, in which he captures it by transforming himself into a self-sufficient mechanism, he is foiled by the ambiguity of love and the duplicity of woman. Molly, a non-Jew, becomes the image of the calcified exterior world which refuses eroticism its free expression. Leopold Bloom is confronted by the problem of Molly, the problem of a world which is not his, a human community to which she could afford him contact if she were not actively engaged in isolating him from it. Bloom's fate is not an enviable one.

It brings us to the core of the western dilemma, but it provides no solution, no liberation, either for the human community or for the Jew. Devotion to a faith, in this case the Jewish faith, cannot show the West its way out of the tunnel into which it has wandered, and eroticism loses its effect except in the form of dreams. What remains is the word, this world that the artist creates not to forget God but to defy Him, a world that interposes between man and God an inoperative dramaturgy. In *Ulysses* Joyce took an inventory of the imagination. This seeming way out is no more than a loophole, and just as its triumph is proclaimed this counterweight to the indifference of God and nature turns out to be no more than an evasion, an admission of defeat. The imaginary is a substitute world and the West has lived by substitutes, ravaging reality without attaining it.

To acquire the status of outsider Joyce had to immerse himself in the turgid waters of a civilization in search at the same time of its sources and its possible destinies. It was his own desire to live abroad. His exile gave him the distance he required from this Occident whose relationship with reality he wanted to explore: the reality to which he came with love and violence, only to find it evanescent. *Ulysses* may have made it unattainable for him, distracted him from the questions he himself posed, precisely because it was a successful work of art, a diversion in the long wait, a consolation in defeat. For if the literary work is to be self-sufficient, if beyond the real, the contingent, beyond particularisms, beyond the ambiguity of love and the inadequacy of imagination it is to constitute the only solid block, the only invention of which man is capable without reference to God or nature, it must, to be truly effective, be a work that is absolute and perfect, where the word is invented and denied, dies and is reborn at the will of man, who, finally, is raised to the rank of creator.

Finnegans Wake was to be his definitive work, marking the defeat and victory of the West. Without referring to nature, as the builders of cathedrals had done, without the despairing cry of prayer of the last mystics, the artist, no longer a "young man" but an adult, no longer the one who receives, absorbs and understands but he who affirms and conquers, this artist was to proclaim the reign of the word, man's creation, in the kingdom of man. Nothing must be left to chance, there must be no slip-ups, no acceptance of a provisional victory, nothing dependant on what was relative or ephemeral. At the end of a forced march during which Joyce exhausted all the resources of the West — myths, legends, dialects, languages and knowledge — this exile, who had always refused to accept either the western empire or the marginality of Ireland, found a title for his "work in progress": a wake for the dead. His discovery is inscribed on the cover. The West cannot be reborn through the madness of a single man, even the most obstinate of geniuses. The artist cannot create reality. He can only sit at the wake of a vast and grandiose enterprise which has failed to bring man into tune with life.

To the extent to which the work is definitive, this recapitulation of civilization, this world of contradictory directions, crossways, mazes, paths leading only to a wake for the dead, is a climax; but it is also a dead-end. This definitive work, this self-sufficient world, this solitary rock has no need of readers to invade, debase and drag it back to the domain of the relative. This work, which refuses to be reduced to a function of mediation, denies not the possibility of a relationship with reality through the dramaturgy of art, but the very place of art in western civilization. If the written work does not communicate, its object disappears. Faced with the indifference of God, the artist who proclaims the empire of man merely writes his own indifference large. Joyce the Occidental, finding himself in a waste land after having explored so many avenues leading to reality, each ending in a closed door, makes the free choice of becoming a nomad, but succeeds only in erecting a monument in which he himself is prisoner, demanding in the folly of his pride the right to solitude, that foretaste of death. Is it possible to carry further such a task?

In its most advanced forms western literature is still stimulated by the experiment of Joyce. Samuel Beckett, his compatriot and secretary, mistrusts the arrogant lessons of his predecessor. If he had been content to play disciple he himself would have been powerless. He had the strength neither to refuse this adventure nor to pursue it, for he suspected the impasse to which it led. He chose to pass by on the side, to take a parallel course. To escape the insoluble contradiction between word and meaning he found a detour. He deliberately draws a line between his own emotion and his verbal style. He does not write in a language that is personally his. He lives out his exile within language itself; and through this deliberate detachment, across a distance arbitrarily and consciously established, he explores the limits of expression and, above all, the resources of dramaturgy. He draws back from the fascinating and terrifying example of Joyce. He has realized, he who tried with Joyce to translate *Finnegans Wake,* that this structure built by man's pride proves his inability to equal God by opposing to His indifference a universe of the imagination, self-sufficient and perhaps as indifferent as God.

This monument, so negligible compared with the intention that lay behind it, is revealed as a new form of dramaturgy. The conclusion becomes inevitable: the West cannot free itself from theatre as a mediator. Beckett uses the theatre not as an instrument of consolation or escape but as a tool of elucidation, an interrogation of its own nature and limitations. Through this theatrical investigation of dramaturgy the fate of western man, which consists of an endless wait for the coming of reality, is pathetically exposed.

I remember the first night of *Waiting for Godot* in Paris. The audience, noisy and rebellious, tried to shout down this revelation of the sickness of their civilization, which, in its very triumphs, finds no way out of its dilemma. Moreover, man's faculty for postponing tragedy is such that these plays, which were intended to deny the effectiveness of theatre as mediation, quickly became a new form of dramaturgy. The theatre, in other words, is not yet dead. In its progress toward reality the West reabsorbs its own negations. On this endless road it transforms each forced halt into a refuge. To speak of the pain of waiting makes waiting tolerable; what a blessing this theatre is, after all, and how far from being "absurd"! Is this long meditation on death not a timid prayer for life? What has been called the theatre of the absurd is in fact no less than a return to the theatre, for to deny theatre in a dramatic work is to seek a more effective theatre.

Beckett was not alone in his undertaking. Marginal figures who, for a variety of reasons, wrote in an impersonal language and kept their distance from their mode of expression, had their own forebodings about the weakness of the theatre, and notions of its possibilities. Its form must be renewed. Ionesco, Adamov, de Ghelderode, Arrabal were successors to a whole constellation of pre-war writers who, clustered around a Germanic world that had never been able to become an empire, were aware of the fragility of cultural expression and the ineffectiveness of theatrical mediation. Broch denounced *Kitsch*, and Canetti saw the emergence of the threat of levelling which the best-equipped libraries in the world were powerless to resist. Peter Weiss, who has since exploited these fears in popular form, has said in his journal that he has only one fatherland: the German language. But the post-war Parisian playwrights could not accept a language of fatherland. For them, the French tongue, that cast-off of a mythical universality which appeared more and more fictitious, could only be a land of exile.

Ionesco's approach to language was a direct one. If the theatre lacks brilliance is it not because words have become inanimate objects, with no luminosity? Where has life been frittered away, and where is the light that gave words their brilliance? He set himself systematically, as a detached observer, a foreigner, to taking apart an encrusted

55

mechanism. Men and women meet. They speak but say nothing. Instead of expressing thought, words provide it with a mask. They serve, not as instruments for attaining reality nor even for describing aspects of it, but for concealing its absence, putting off the moment of admitting its unattainability. Words are no longer even theatrical. Language has become inanimate, like dice, and there are no more surprises in the results of each throw, for chance has been abolished. The game has become ludicrous. If what is being concealed is emptiness, the dissimulation is not amusing. Yet Ionesco achieves his purpose. What he writes is theatre. By depriving words of their normal sense he gives them back mobility. And behind his clichés he reveals the drama of communication, this relationship that people try consciously and deliberately to establish, for he illustrates the absence and impossibility of immediate, direct and spontaneous contact. Yet if men and women are victims of non-communication it is not because they have nothing to say, but rather because of the ineffectiveness of their tools of dramatization. His theatre is shattered, to be sure, by invasions of violence, but the fragility of language also suffers as words disintegrate under the weight of clichés. Propaganda transforms speed into slogans. By making us aware of these things Ionesco, beyond the ludicrous, gives words a new strength. He reveals their hidden, unused resources. This is precisely what consoles us. For if words are stifled under the weight of appearances, all that is needed is an emotive will, a poetic intent, for them to rediscover their original purity. Ionesco's innocence, his astonishment at words, the seriousness with which he approaches them, lead us back past the ravages of banality to the innocence, perhaps masked and latent, of the word.

Pinter has gone further in this dialectic between expression and what it conceals. Here revelation comes through breaking the mask. And the theatre provides a superb field of action for this confrontation, for through the theatre this negation of an older theatre grown ineffectual can best take place. Pinter's solution is not a direct rapport with reality but a new dramaturgy.

The proponents of the new novel, instead of approaching reality from the side of dramatization, try to adopt reality's structures by rebuilding them patiently, coldly, systematically. They do attempt to renew the dramatization of the tale. The author does not withdraw, but pretends to stand outside his story; he hides and forces the reader into a similar game of masks. To rediscover a relationship with reality he dresses it in an artifice of his own invention. He succeeds only in touching the masks under which he has himself concealed it.

This game is quickly exhausted through awareness of the rules, and other ways are sought for. It is not in describing the visible that the mystery of reality can be pierced. On the contrary, this merely deepens the mystery. If reality is not the world and the men who inhabit it, if it is within us, we have only to plunge into this unknown sea to find our harmony. Though existing dramatizations no longer succeed in establishing a relationship with the unknown, the incommunicable, with God, we create a new device to appease our anguish before the void, and generate a fresh satisfaction for western pride. We proclaim that the unknown is within us, and that in ourselves we can explore its shores. What began as a tool of artistic exploration is transformed into therapy for troubled souls. Little by little the number of patients has grown. Lay priests are paid high fees for listening to the ever-repeated tale of a childhood ever-reinvented. There is a considerable distance between the discoveries of Freud and the games of confession. Psychoanalysts quickly became stage-directors of a dramatic game for individuals who agree to be actors and spectators at once, on condition that the vigilant eye of the witness reassures them of the usefulness of the game. This dramatization is also petering out. The self does not contain infinite resources, and one grows tired of a theatre whose final effectiveness remains uncertain.

New York has been in the forefront of this kind of individual theatre, where each educated bourgeois feels the need to return to his childhood. Here the game becomes a little shrill, when it does not fizzle out in the ludicrous. There is more and more talk of the psychodrama, of group analysis. It is no longer enough to be a solitary spectacle, one joins a game in which each player makes a show of his life. Under the impression that he is revealing his life and baring its secrets, he does no more than dramatize the everyday and the banal, because he is cut off from any beyond, any reality, and the traditional mediations no longer work.

This introversion is a process that quickly reaches its limits. Those who persist in saying that the resources of the self are inexhaustible are driven to put the self out of order, to tamper with it. To be sure, drugs and hallucinogens are not inventions of our age. Many poets used them in the past. But they were reserved for an elite, and their virtues of interior dramatization were reserved for those discontented with existing mediations, just as the intimate diary was the literary form affected by those who could do no more than dramatize their own lives. In an age when individual dramatization is no longer reserved for an elite, when psychoanalysis invades a field where only artists ventured before, drugs have become the last frontier of self-dramatization. Faced with the unattainability of reality, we create a world of forgetfulness, or one that makes reality's absence bearable. Self-dramatization through drugs, of course, leads with increasing frequency to a need for disguise. The spectacle of oneself is not satisfying for long, because an essential element of theatre is lacking: the spectator, the witness. One covers oneself with heteroclite garments and goes walking in groups, affirming in the face of the multitude that this is indeed a spectacle. The spectator also must affirm his presence, through anger or laughter, or this particular theatre would quickly go bankrupt.

With structuralism, the inefficacy of existing dramatizations has been recognized on a further level. In order to understand the failure of a civilization to establish a direct relationship with reality some have begun to search in so-called primitive civilizations for certain constant factors, laws that reassure by telling us the failure is universal. The mediating power of language is denied. It exists on its own, with its own laws and structures. It is a given fact, like nature. Man is able to intervene in its processes only insofar as he understands its mechanism and is able to manipulate it. Language exists apart from man. It can exist in a latent form in his absence. Because of this fact the artist does not establish a relationship with reality but explores a world whose existence precedes his own. This world is language. In societies where faith governed gestures and actions there was the affirmation of a hidden world with its own rules and laws. There God did battle with Satan, and each had his sbirros and angels. That world was a reflection of our own, and gave it coherence, a beginning and an end. Thus when God goes into hiding we seek for other kinds of coherence that can be classified and categorized. Here the western mind can exercise its logic and affirm its concepts. It proceeds to reveal, or pretend to reveal, the structures of the world. The world is without a sense of intention and not penetrated by the will of God. Laws exist without apparent reason, possessing their own coherence; reality is only a reflection of those laws. If the key to the enigma can be discovered and the structure revealed, we shall come to know the laws of reality and its coherence. From this moment the relationship with reality becomes a matter for scientific investigation. Life has its laws. No one imposed them or invented them. Man has only to understand and adapt to them in order to control them.

The world is there, and man need only understand it in order to find his place in it: there is no call for mediation or for a direct relationship with reality. Here we have the supreme attempt at dramatization. This language, which is not man's invention and not married to the movement of life, is a mediation which denies itself, as the theatre of the absurd is a dramatization in aid of a refusal of drama.

Christianity sought to discover divine laws and apply them to human societies. Structuralism, which is its mirror counterpart, abolishes mediation in a self-sufficient world. Structures are there to be discovered, and hierarchies exist which man is compelled to obey. Consequently we can discover and classify the laws of reality. Thus we invent a world which replaces mediation. Except that this invented world is still a mediation, though under false pretences, and is imposed with their own consent on men cut off from reality. When we can no longer live reality we classify it.

The new techniques of communication have developed too quickly to be an adequate replacement for mediations grown ineffective. There is a certain distance between man and the image he has created. It is not illuminated from within, like an ancient painting, by an emotive charge. Not being integrated into man's interior space, the image becomes mechanized, a kind of non-figurative art. It neither interprets reality nor reflects nature. It acquires an autonomous existence and consequently can not serve as mediator, for it has contact neither with man nor with reality. A bastard dramatization, it frustrates man's search for reality, offering instead second-hand dreams, fragile and ephemeral. By their multiplicity, these means of communication heighten man's appetite for reality. If they replace it, the price they exact is a half-conscious servitude to artifice. Man resigns himself to artifice because he no longer knows in the name of what he could refuse it.

The young observe that traditional mediations no longer work even for their parents, and that constant changes of fashions in dress or music fail to cover the void they are meant to hide. The young are aware that they live in a world of ephemera; and that while reality escapes them life remains a free and uncertain gift, which in its turn will be stolen from them. The thief remains anonymous. If what is essential is constantly vanishing, anything we propose can only seem to them laughable and inadequate. Whence the strident, angry, impotent cry, filled with blind hope: participation. If the young demand to be involved in decisions it is because they clumsily wish to have a part in the creation of reality. The multiplication of means of communication has hastened their divorce from the world. In the absence of rapport with the real, communication is a tantalizing repetition of the emptiness, leading to an attempted return to sources through anarchy, violence, disappointed love and fallen hopes. They reject the dramatizations that have nourished the West: ideologies, conquests, mysticisms without God. Yet their quest is profoundly religious, and just as profoundly erotic. They see nothing to be saved in a civilization that has finally banished God and mechanized sex. They feel hemmed in. They can fall back on neither a primal Orient nor a new dramatization. At best they may dramatize their youth and their revulsion while waiting for a new statue of God to be raised, one before which they can again bow down.

When an Egyptian critic, some twenty years ago, wrote a study on the literary style of the Koran, he quickly had cause to regret it. Every scholar of Al Azhar condemned his essay as blasphemy. They were right. The Koran is the word of God, not a model of style. It is made up of words transmitted to man by Mohammed and the Angel Gabriel. Sacred words, final dicta. The word was not made flesh. Nothing is farther removed from the sacred word than a poetic image. And God's word cannot have a style, not even the highest style. For the word is. It is not a mediation that has acquired autonomy. It is an instrument for direct contact with God. Literature, it follows, loses all sovereignty. It is no more than a reference to the final word. It is no more than the profane use of a word addressed to God, or addressed by God to man.

Equally rigorous, equally jealous, is the concern of the Jews not to profane the Lechon Hakodech, the sacred language. In Eastern Europe pious Jews forbade the debasement of Hebrew through everyday use. For that there was Yiddish. In my school our Hebrew professor reminded us constantly to take care the sacred book did not fall to the floor. If by ill luck the Bible touched our feet we hastened to press on it the kiss of sanctification. Literature never grew autonomous in the Jewish tradition. It is no more than the apologia or commentary on a word that has been laid down. The language, thanks to this consecration, has kept its innocence, and its vigour has never been diminished. In the diaspora Jews did not speak Hebrew. When the Israelis made of it a language for daily use they discovered its inexhaustible resources. Hebrew had not calcified. A few westernisms sufficed to modernize it. The fact that Hebrew no longer has the Bible as its sole reference may cut off the profane language from its sacred origins. The Arab tongue has been marked for a long time by the juxtaposition of sacred and profane. Perhaps Arabs speak in dialects so as unconsciously to conserve the perfection of the Koranic language. Arabic grammar is an accumulation of subtleties and refinements. The language itself is immutable. All its possibilities for flexibility are concentrated in the grammatical commentary. This grammar is not intended to preserve the purity of the language; grammar is superimposed, an autonomous body. This mathematics of the wits transforms words into ciphers. And in the Talmud this same subtle game is played with phrases from the Bible. In neither case does this gymnastic of the mind result in an abstraction. Words and phrases, like the ornamentation of the mosque or synagogue, are not transformed into conceptual structures. The Kabbala interprets not the world but the number. It notes the enigma of a sovereign force without reducing it to magic.

Without ever ceasing to refer back to the immutable Koranic rock, Arabic grammar and poetry finally won their autonomy in the course of the centuries. Their ornamental structure does not pretend to attain the heights of the sacred. At their best, they testify to its superiority; at worst they fall into futility. In other words, literature at its very birth is marked with the seal of the marginal. The sacred word reduces all others, especially those identical to it, to the domain of the superfluous. It is through the sacred word that we come to what is essential. It has been written once and for all. The rest is only commentary and decor. Thus it is not surprising that Arabic poetry, when translated, appears extremely commonplace, and that its original classic verse-form follows quasi-geometric laws of rhyme and rhythm. Words are soporifics. The pleasure they produce is immediate, spontaneous. They capture the sensuality of a relationship with the everyday and embellish it. And when they do not achieve sensuality they often end in empty rhetoric, with no reference to the sacred and no roots in experience. In its decadence Arab literature was a decor built on sand. It floundered in the byways of futility. The same applies, more strikingly, to music. There is no musical heritage in the Arab world, and Jewish music belongs to the synagogue. Song consists, on the one hand, of prayer or the recitation of texts from the Bible or the Koran or, on the other, of a spontaneous expression, direct and immediate, of a physical sensation which music amplifies and sets free.

Bach still lives because his work was in the domain of music itself, separated from direct and spontaneous expression, and capable of being transmitted from one generation to the next. We know that in the palaces of the Caliphs, singers male and female enlivened the nights of princes and sovereigns. I listen to a recording of Oum Koulthoum. His long, improvised chant, interminably taken up and begun afresh, touches our own sensitivity, for it is the product of another sensitivity that flowers in an immediate, spontaneous way. There is a sensual satisfaction in this music. Transplanted into surroundings that are not its natural habitat its melody becomes theatre. This music without a history then becomes pure exoticism, or, for those who feel it as an original rite, evokes nostalgia. What makes Oum Koulthoum uniquely precious is that this is beyond doubt the last voice to achieve a harmony between song and experience. Abdul Wahab, who pilfered from occidental music to adapt it to the taste of circles that were superficially westernized, was among the first to Levantinize Arab music. Of course it becomes less authentic in the process. It no longer satisfies the same needs. Arab music, which has no past, is vulnerable to the assault of the West through popular music. Already Asmahan, Sabah and Feirouz can be heard singing tangos with a dash of oriental sauce.

In literature the renewal was the product of a meeting between Arabic poetry and the West. In New York and Sao Paolo, Christians from Lebanon recall in their Mijhar, their emigration, that they belong to the Orient. Gibran, Naima, Abu Madhi were doubly liberated from the Arab tradition. For them the Koran was no more than a literary reference. And the distant Orient (often idealized in an Occident in which they sometimes did not want, sometimes were unable, to be integrated) became for them a refuge they invented as they went along. In their poetry the West has battered its way into the Orient, with weapons and baggage trains. Arab literature, when it does not fall into empty rhetoric, attaching itself stubbornly to traditions with no surviving link to experience, borrows its methods from the West without achieving their function of mediation. When rhetoric is dramatized the word becomes a mediation, but in relation to what? In relation to another rhetoric. So that political and intellectual life becomes littered with invective that has no reference to reality. Anathema, in the absence of the sacred, becomes arbitrary. The sacred has taken refuge in hidden places, protected by demagogues who exploit it and fanatics who are incapable of living in accordance with it.

In Israel the Jews are beginning to feel the effects of this separation of the sacred and the profane. The Hebrew word has become an everyday thing. There is no guarantee that teaching the Bible as a history book and as literature can preserve it from rhetoric, for the Jews have entered a western world, built by themselves in a given physical space, without their language having passed the test of a long cohabitation of the eternal and the ephemeral. Will the Bible become a book of reference, reduced, except for a minority, to the level of what is merely relative?

Jews and Moslems stand before the same dilemma. They can not safeguard the virtues of their languages without renouncing the present. Nowadays reality invades and lays siege to them from the outside. What was immediate becomes the object of a quest. The tools they have are not forged to perform the mediations that have become necessary. A return to the primal Orient becomes doubly impossible, for the past is a reminder of their failure, and the present subjects them to a triumphant West. Yet how can they adopt the mediations that have been the tools of the West at a time when these seem of doubtful efficacy? The West has at least the consolation of having built a great civilization, and the further consolation of being able to live off its accumulated riches, an inexhaustible cultural treasure that is its heritage. The Orient has consumed its treasures as it went along. It has snatched at life, exhausting it in an erotic embrace. Now it can live its sensuality only under a mask made in Hollywood. Fidelity to its sources would today be a lie. What is left to it is rhetoric; and any attempt to turn inward toward itself can only be a fanatic's dream. Should it forget itself? This would be to accept an Occident that is unsure of its own goals, despite its triumphs. For the tourist on the shores of the Tigris there are no castles to visit, no paintings to contemplate. Haroun al Rashid is the name of a street frequently occupied by groups of demonstrators. The name itself is a mockery. Men in anger lose themselves in the crowd. They scream, they do not sing for joy. Frustrated of their past,

65

their present is unbearable, and the future they are offered is a borrowed one, a lie. Will the cry again become Word? Or will the dream-machine bring total oblivion?

Object and Shadow

The sentinels who search every visitor for weapons are holding a man by the shoulders. He yells, "I have cleansed my honour!" In his hand he grips a bloodstained dagger. This scene is common in the Maidan, the red-light district of Baghdad. Men come from far away to immolate a sister or cousin turned prostitute.

One of the Arabic words meaning honour, *Ardh,* also means wife. There is an overlap between one's honour and the woman one has chosen to engender life. Love or jealousy do not enter into the matter; the woman who sins transgresses, not a moral law, but the laws of life.

Yet the Koran does allow one submerged force into the otherwise bleak and deprived life of the nomad: pleasure is legitimate and woman is its most perfect source. The paradise of the Koran is filled with women, and Arab poets have never tired of celebrating their sensuality. Mohammed opposed a practice that was current in his day, called *Al Wa'ad,* according to which newborn baby girls were buried alive. The prophet enjoined the faithful to let all babies live: God would ensure that they were fed.

Islam's attitude to women has oscillated between these two extremes. Man's companion is a useless extra mouth to feed; she is also the supreme source of pleasure.

On Friday evening, to celebrate the coming of the Sabbath, Jews chant the virtues of Eshet Hail, the courageous woman. Wife and mother, but no stimulant to concupiscence, she is venerated, yet her place in the synagogue is in the balcony. And when God decides to heap his blessings on Abraham, Sarah conceives a child despite her age. The miracle is life, and it is produced through the operation, the mediation of woman. This life is a gift of God, a free gift. It depends on His superior and arbitrary will. Abraham knows this so well that he never questions the fact that Isaac's fate, his life or death, are not Abraham's to dispose of.

As long as man obeys God's will, however arbitrary it may be, his existence is not stained with guilt. Living is neither sin nor expectant waiting; it is a gift, a happiness to be protected. God demands the sacrifice of Isaac only to show how easily the gift can be withdrawn if man's alliance with Him is not sealed by obedience. If Abraham, the father of humanity, consents to the sacrifice of his only son (that is, to the conclusion of the story even before it begins) then God will revoke his demand for the sacrifice. History will be determined by the alliance; it will be the work of man obeying God's will. Nature, on the other hand, will be sacrificed. To seal his alliance with God, Abraham (who was ready to sacrifice the future of the race) certainly does not hesitate to sacrifice the ram. Father and son unite under the protective scrutiny of God to defend life against a nature that is hostile. The scourge will strike if man betrays the alliance and leaves his chosen path. It is not a blind force that reduces him to powerlessness, leaving him no recourse but the cry of anger or despair. If man's destiny is not absurd, life in its fragility appears as the supreme good, and enjoyment is not reprehensible. God gives life by the intercession of woman, and man protects this precious gift. Thus life is threatened not only by a superior will which can stop its course at any moment, but also by the weakness of the mediator, woman. The divine will is final wisdom, but woman, being human, is weak and can alter the original purity of the source, especially as she is the object of concupiscence. Neither East nor West has solved the enigma: the act of creation is also the incarnation of extreme pleasure; the act that creates life can

68

also exhaust life's source in utter loss. Woman is the focus of this contradiction, a double being who can be the source of life or its ruin. It falls to man, who defends this life in the midst of a hostile nature, to safeguard its purity, and especially that of the instrument through which it is perpetuated. To succeed is he not bound to reduce woman to an object? She, who gives birth and offers pleasure, must not have a will of her own. Otherwise the role of man as guardian of life would itself be riddled with ambiguity. He protects and guides woman; she owes him submission and obedience. When the roles are divided this way the woman who transgresses the law unites herself with forces that are destructive of life; she seals her own fate, and must herself be destroyed.

Prostitutes reward man for his work as protector of life, but they stamp that life with the sign of death if they are not simply objects, if they are recognized as part of a family or are permitted a name, an identity.

As a young student in the law faculty in Baghdad I could not hide my surprise when the professor explained to us certain articles of Al Majjala, the code extracted by the Ottomans from the Koranic law. "The reason woman is considered to be eternally under-age," he told me, "is that regardless of her years she is the victim of her own weakness and uncontrollable impulses." Islam does not give her the right to marry an infidel, yet a Moslem man may marry a Christian or Jewish woman without the latter being obliged to embrace his faith. They need only procreate, for the man, who is responsible for the future of his children, will make sure that they are raised as Moslems. The Jews are less confident of male supremacy, since throughout history the Jewish man has not been master in his society. The child is recognized through his mother. Christianity dissociated this basic equation of birth and life by giving both a merely symbolic sense. What fails to satisfy the mind is transformed into theatre and applies, in any case, only in appearance. Jesus is the son of God. The purity of his birth is not a

69

material thing, and need not be confirmed by any law of nature. All children who are born can get along without the material confirmation of their origin, for they are reborn by the dramatic act called baptism. Their souls thus saved, they become children of God.

The Orient encountered a basic ambiguity: the association of the act of creation with pleasure. Procreation, besides being just that, happens also to be the ultimate happiness that can be experienced through an act. It is reality seized by the body in a union where life appears as its own fulfilment, its immediate accomplishment, a self-consumption in the act, in which a complete exhausting of reality is inextricable from pleasure. The Orient has not been able to reconcile the two terms of the contradicition: the preservation of life in its purity, and the preservation of what has been lived in its total exhaustion. The Christian West chose a process of dissociation, relegating to a double theatre the dream of a reality experienced in time, and the total exhausting of the moment seized in immediacy. The supreme expression of femininity is no longer fecundity, for God chooses to offer His son to the world through a virgin. And this son is a martyr to reality. In order that life may not be exhausted in the here and now, a supreme theatre equates the here and now with death. Thus the real is sacrificed — a 'real' whose ambiguity and basic contradiction are denied by the Son of Man. He thereby breaks the continuity of what men have lived; but he will rise from the dead, and what men have lived will be transfigured into theatre. This God, descended to earth, can maintain the link of flesh with man only on condition that man renounce the continuity of what has been lived and accept that all duration is theatrical. Henceforth God's mediators choose the paths of celibacy and virginity. Man must be born twice, once in time and again in an invisible union with the beyond, the two births being of entirely different orders. The first must

70

be inferior, for it is a savage state which is merely a step toward divine purification. Procreation becomes sanctified by an act that escapes contingency. Sexual pleasure is not a consolation, not a sanctification of the moment, but a sin, transgression against a higher order — an order which denies time and experience, which transfigures death into theatre and life into a necessary but savage and passing condition. Pleasure is the necessary evil, making it possible for life (which would otherwise be purely spiritual) to accomplish its purpose despite the fall. Impossible for the woman to be a reward, or for the pleasure she gives to be a taste of paradise. She is the agent of a lower order, an ally of Satan. She is a distraction to man in his noble work of building a world in which God will dwell as conqueror. Of course, love exists, and sex as well. The charms of woman are acknowledged and sung. But this is a courtly love, and woman is reduced to a symbol of femininity that cannot be touched by the sin of sex.

Western literature is one long description of the misery that is womanhood, reduced to an instrument of pleasure, rejected and idealized at the same time. Sexual pleasure is punished, except when it takes the form of a deliberate plunge into the depths because of one's despair at the unattainability of the plenitude reserved for followers of the mystic quest. Suffering inflicted or experienced is thus no longer an ascetic way which celebrates the silencing of the body for the duration of its journey to the beyond, but a price we guilty humans pay for the right to sexual pleasure. The body is never given freely, for physical enjoyment is neglect of a higher order which has declared it to be a sin.

The West has recognized the autonomy of woman by making her a divided being. She is an object, an instrument of pleasure, without ceasing to be the virgin, pure image of an ethereal beauty that rises above the everyday world. She is immunized against sin, and finally becomes pure symbol — an image of femininity. She has been elevated to a kind of theatre, succeeding in living up to her image only if she

71

voluntarily denies her nature and takes virginity as armour against the assaults of base reality. She can become one of two things: object or image.

Yet western literature abounds in subtle feminine characters who are sensual without falling into the role of the scarlet woman. Writers, of course, can reinstate what has been rejected by a society's current mythology. It is natural that women invented by novelists often escape the rigid criteria of this mythology. Otherwise they remain creatures of instinct, who insinuate a certain ambiguity into the ideal of masculinity; or they are incomplete persons who never reach the age of responsibility, who can be ignored with the superior smile of maturity.

The industrial age has projected woman into the working world. In Anglo-Saxon countries the suffragettes have been demanding equality for many years. Society has now granted them certain civil rights. They have been accepted as citizens. They can govern, vote, and manage monies; yet when a man is with them he rushes to open doors, and when they enter a room men stand and offer their chairs. The more woman succeeds in leaving behind her dream existence, the more she achieves the condition of subject – and the more obvious becomes the dichotomy between the actual person and the image. Despite the material freedom she has preached and obtained, the woman-become-citizen grows even more aware of the ubiquitous presence of her own image. The more she appropriates masculine attributes, wearing pants, smoking, drinking . . . the more insistently the symbols of femininity multiply and degenerate in the culture around her.

The mass media popularise these symbols. Thus the flesh-and-blood, accessible woman has not dissipated the image men have of femininity. Only the symbols have changed. Reality has exploded the myths of virginity and purity, yet the act of sex is still tainted with sin, and sensual joy is hampered by taboos. The old myth, grown ineffective, has not given way to reality but opened the way to a new myth. For sex itself has become theatre.

The western world is invaded by eroticism, but it is a theatrical eroticism. The photo of the film star leads, not to sensual joy with a living woman, but to another photo of another star, more daring and provocative than the first. Excitation through images is heightened not by the inaccessibility of the real woman, but by other images which make access to reality less and less desirable. Sex is more widely allowed, but because it has become theatrical it has become mechanized. And as a free citizen, woman is as vulnerable as man to the assault of reality. The new erotic dramaturgy leaves woman no recourse beyond a mechanised sexuality. And now woman herself takes part in the elaboration of her own myth. In this new theatre of the erotic she herself manufactures the images and symbols of a new dramaturgy. The myth of masculinity changes correspondingly. It is no longer the creation of man trying to justify his right to dominate woman, it is the creation of woman dreaming of a super-sexuality that might deliver her from the oppressive limitations of mechanised sex. Women's magazines construct and elaborate this myth of masculinity.

Ten or twenty years ago these magazines were guide-books to seduction. Woman, the object, found in them lessons on how to "charm" or "enchant". Her means were magical, for her powers were not the expression of a manifest and authentic power, but of some hidden force. Then charm gave way to sex-appeal. Seductiveness grew less vague and somehow measurable, even if there was no definition of sex-appeal. Now the mystery was no longer feminine but sexual. And people set to work to define it. Products were launched on the market to emphasise attractions that grew more and more obvious. The mystery grew thin. Having gained equality woman retained no weapons other than those of a surface femininity. Had her powers grown more real because they no longer relied on magic? The myth of the

73

super-woman is the answer to that of the superman. But it has become evident that neither man nor woman can live up to this sexuality that is the essence of their dream of happiness. For the woman, her "charm" is no longer a weapon to subdue the man, to reduce his domination by adapting herself to his powers. It is a definition of her being, an identity. It is, of course, possible to define an identity in terms of myth, but sexuality is by its nature not a myth, and the woman who gives it this rank becomes a constant victim of her dream of femininity.

Betty Friedan has described the disenchantment of the woman who would like her femininity to be simultaneously an autonomy, an identity and a kind of magic, combined in what she calls the feminine mystique. It is following this sort of disenchantment that the myth of "woman as sexual force" became detached from "woman as reality." In the process of creating a mythical image of masculinity woman creates her own myth. She can only fall into frustration and melancholy as she measures the gap between the masculine myth and the man she marries or frequents, or the gap between the feminine myth and the woman that she is. In his turn the man feels dwarfed beside the giant of his woman's dreams. And she, for him, is now no more than the image she creates of herself. As he takes in his arms a living woman, is he perhaps embracing a shadow? Is he anything more than the victim of a spectre?

If pornography invades the mass media, if consumption of it has become everyday, and if the erotic image pervades advertising, it is because eroticism, in this world where masculinity and femininity have become theatre, has been transformed into a spectacle. Pornography becomes inoffensive, for it does not dramatise reality but rather dresses up a dream, an image of reality. There is no exit from this situation for western man. The mechanisation of sex is pushed to the extreme, accompanied by a search for the ultra-padded hideaway, the escape to heavy-lidded oblivion. The diversity of sexual experience divorced from emotional

74

attachment leads to a sensation-hunt, using exotic methods. Indicatively, we no longer speak of "perverts," but "sexual minorities." Fashion itself follows and sometimes anticipates the practices of certain social levels. Women's dress is now boyish, now mini-skirted, now hung with chains. The mass media go through an enormous number of faintly-disguised images evocative of homosexuality, sadism and masochism.

In its search for a lost shock-effect, pornography is no longer a stimulus, a provocation, nor even an expression of mania. It is fantasy completely out of contact with reality. On the bookstands of railway stations, airports and drug-stores of North America there is a plethora of pocket-books of a new variety. In the new pulp novel we find nothing but sadists, masochists, voyeurs and homosexuals of every shape and kind. To be sure "sexual minorities" have always existed, and bought under the counter books designed for them. But this new merchandise is not primarily designed to satisfy special tastes. It brings to a wide spectrum of readers fantasies which, under the guise of realism, lead to escapism. This brutal sex, in which experimentation seems to promise a rediscovery of sensuality, in fact takes the reader further from any real desire for satisfaction. There may be, of course, in this lingering over the descriptions of latent obsessions, some liberation from an inner darkness. But the illumination is not an embracing of reality. It accepts the rejection of that reality, in the illusion of having recaptured an easy conscience. The brutality of these fantasies makes their escapism less obvious, but it confines the reader within his own body, allowing him to avoid the terrifying ambiguity of a relationship with another human being. Now he can exercise total authority over a woman reduced to an image: an authority all the greater because this image-woman may be insatiable and perverse. At its extreme this fantasy leads to onanism as a way of life. Man, terrified by the Other, by the external world, deserts it willingly, under the impression that he can possess it by transforming it into fantasy. Thus pornography is no longer that glaucous water that drips from the sub-basements of consciousness, but a fiction that dramatises what is intolerable about reality, de-fusing it by reducing it to a function of the imagination, neutralising its effects. It is not surprising that sexual crime has noticeably decreased in Denmark since the open sale of pornographic works was legalised.

As adolescents we exchanged forbidden publications that we obtained through the complicity of a bookseller. They fell into two categories. First there was a Lebanese magazine which had assumed the mission of defending virtue by displaying the evil mechanisms of vice: salacious stories, illustrations of half-naked women. It was an imitation and in large measure a translation of similar French magazines. The other category consisted of books printed in ancient characters on yellowed paper. I remember one which bore the title *The Old Man's Return to Youth*. The title and the first page gave a deceptive impression of the contents. One was almost led to believe it was a text on law or theology. The first part, moreover, confirmed this impression: recipes, concoctions and advice to help perform the sex act in the best ways and derive the maximum benefit from it. The book ended with a few stories calculated to arouse those unaffected even by aphrodisiacs. It seems that a certain caliph had ordered the composition of this treatise on sexual savoir-faire for distribution to the men in his court. He was disturbed at the excessive preference for young boys among members of his entourage.

In Arab countries, traditionally and in practice, homosexuality, no less prevalent than in the West, is superficially just another variety of sexual pleasure. It satisfies those who because of circumstances have no access to women. It completes the joy of those who, having tasted abundantly of sexual pleasures, seek to add new spice to the experience. On the surface this homosexuality is quite distinct from the

76

relationships of man and woman, and thus should change them in no way. Yet I remember the outrageously made-up face of an adolescent boy walking in the red-light district of Baghdad. He was the constant butt of gibes from the visitors. Other boys of his age, fresh from the prostitutes' beds, insulted him furiously, trying to pinch his buttocks or his cheeks. For them nothing could have been more humiliating than the spectacle he created. Reduced to a woman's state, deprived of his masculinity, the boy had lost all his manly dignity. Thus homosexuality reproduced — while it accentuated and caricatured — the relationship prevailing between man and woman. Just as woman is dominated and becomes an object, the homosexual relationship is one of domination. When the Other is no longer a woman (who is dominated by definition), the authority exercised by the dominant partner becomes a humiliation. This humiliation, in its turn, by dramatising the element of domination in the man-woman relationship, confirms it. Sensual pleasure is no longer an exchange, and man is confined within a masculinity that dispenses pleasure but is unable to reach out to the Other. Man attempts, by transforming his masculinity into an instrument of power or domination, to open the door of his prison. In the open he meets only his own image, his solitude which will not leave him alone. Pleasure not followed by personal communion is sterile. Then variety becomes the only solution. In a world where woman is absent, pleasure is not a marriage of life and reality but the expression of a power that dominates reality. In its extremity this mode of relationship with the world can explode in political action and violence.

In the West woman is absent, not dominated. She is not an object but an image. Man follows the long road of imagination and fantasy and ends up facing a mirror. Can reality be caught in this mirror? Homosexuality is not the domination of reality by masculine power but, in the absence of woman, a flight from reality, an escape into the self. Narcissus is a touchstone. The western homosexual not only accepts solitude, he arms himself with it. The Other exists only as a dramatisation of the self, and this homosexuality is in fact no more than onanism camouflaged. From Gide to Burroughs, from Jef Last to T. E. Lawrence, western homosexuals who sought to slake in sexuality their thirst for a relationship with the Other, and who despaired of finding in the Occident a woman who was not a shadow-woman, fled to a mythical Orient in which the Other was able to break through the mirror because he appeared in the guise of the Foreigner.

Several American-Jewish novelists, such as Bruce Jay Friedman and Philip Roth, depict woman as a matron who castrates the male, formulates the laws of sacrifice and ensures the observance of taboos, thus depriving man of all sensual joy; so that when he tries, despite prohibitions, to indulge in these pleasures, they have a bitter taste. In the recurring role of Christopher Columbus, Jewish man in a new world ruled by puritanism tries to dominate a reality from which he is not excluded by hostility and persecution. To belong to American society without losing himself, to accept a new form of relationship with reality without abandoning forever the dream of a primal Orient: these are the contradictions he cannot reconcile. Huddled in the surrounding puritanism, he cannot resign himself to it without discomfort, and cannot without irony accept the do-it-yourself theatre called psychoanalysis. He had grown accustomed in central Europe to limiting the area of his domination to his family and his *shtetl*. There he could elaborate on his culture, which isolated him from the outside world. Irony enabled him to accept the fact of the world around him without submitting to it, for his consciousness of his own condition consoled him and even at times made him believe that he was not resigned to it. His restricted domain was illuminated by the ancient Jewish hope. In America his domain is the entire continent. He had only to leave his *shtetl* to become master of it. Leave his *shtetl* and lose himself. A re-assignment of roles takes place. The woman now clings to her son, nourishing him on a past that is receding and growing empty; while the father launches him on an adventure on which he himself has just embarked. The son is caught between two false promises. The adventure leads him not to reality but to the theatrical, and the tradition inflicts on him a groundless sense of guilt. If the traditional laws imposed seem arbitrary to him he should be able to transgress them joyfully. But no, guilt transfixes him, and Judaism is transformed into a puritanism whose victim is the man and whose guardian is the woman as mother. This puritanism is based on no ethic and no faith. In the case of the Jew who succeeds neither in abandoning his past nor accepting a reality that diminishes him, the theatrical becomes a burlesque, and the irony of central Europe is transmuted into black humour. Pleasure and guilt are two sides of the same joke, the same gigantic farce.

It was a long-standing belief in the West that when the social and economic equality of women was established, a long-postponed happiness would be the automatic result. The relationship of man to woman was reduced to its societal factors. Material comfort has only aggravated the feeling of something missing, turning the long wait to despair. What future is there for men and women who embrace but remain inaccessible to each other? The image, ephemeral by nature, loses its precision and efficacy unless it is continually renewed. At this point reality gives a hand to fantasy. Sexual experiment, masochism, sadism . . . prolong the success of a mechanized sexuality whose efficacy is always precarious. And so a setting must be concocted, not just readings from the Marquis de Sade or the *Story of O* but a concrete dramatization of the products of a fevered imagination, in an attempt to capture a sexuality grown evanescent.

The other choice is to curl up inside the self, to make of one's own body the stage of a dramatic game in which one is spectator and actor at once, with no need of outside intervention. Enter drugs. But they are a poor substitute for life; the resultant exasperation tends to break out in violence; society is declared sick and life a hopeless mess.

Social evolution in the Arab countries has been equally unsuccessful in resolving the fundamental contradiction confronting men and women: the conflict between the transmission of life and its exhaustion in pleasure. They have chosen, as between the absolute and the relative, to eliminate the latter and reduce woman, the ambiguous being, to the status of object. But social evolution has begun to allow her a certain autonomy. The rights she demands are those western woman already enjoys. Social evolution in the Near East does not lead to a new and original relationship between man and woman but to an alignment with and resignation to the prevailing style in the West. Men in the Orient resist the process, and one sees Marxist Moslems among the most fervent opponents of women's liberation. Beyond the spheres of belief and ideology they feel confusedly that the westernization of their customs deprives them of their last defence against a world in which man's relationship with reality is mediated by dramaturgy. By dominating woman, oriental man affirms his grasp of reality, but in dominating her he reduces her to an object and his reality is diminished to the vanishing point. There is a younger generation who would like at the same time to dominate woman, so as to be masters of life, and to admit her equality, so as to be able to live that life. This confusion leads to malaise, and political explosions and violence are indications of its seriousness. Precisely as the West reaches its impasse, questioning the very validity of its civilisation and the options and basic choices underlying it, the Semitic East, despite its inner resistance, despite the guardians of an empty tradition who prolong their losing and hopeless battle, is starting down the path beaten by the West. The East is resigned to its failure in face of the rise of a technological civilisation. It adopts western processes and, as the price for abandoning its primal options, it has the consolation of taking lessons in efficiency.

The dream of building a civilisation in which the spontaneity of life need not be dampened by a feeling of pervasive guilt; a civilisation in which birth is not stamped with the sign of death, where daily fulfillment is an answer, perhaps a defiant answer, to death, where daily life is not transformed into a slow waiting tainted by fascination with that fatal end: the dream of such a civilisation is fading. If there is dread of the consumer civilisation, it is because it grinds out nothing but images, and reality slips through man's fingers. There is still a tenacious, savage will that man and woman be allowed to live daily in touch with reality, to taste pleasure despite all taboos, to proclaim happiness and laugh at sin, leaving behind the burden of guilt. Death comes in any case. It ends as winner, and no civilisation has escaped its reign. Only a few isolated individuals, exiles from civilisation, escape death's domination, accepting each day as a rebirth. Doubtless they merely postpone the final deadline. But when it comes, they do not depart as losers. They do not submit before their time.

Groups and Communities

At the corner of the main street and the covered market, the café was crowded to overflowing. Most of the clients were street-porters, and they gathered there in droves at the end of the day. Then a few snatches of song, beginning almost as murmurs, could be heard, gradually gaining confidence. These tired men pursued their chants as if they were telling secrets, paying no attention to the discord they created with competing voices from neighbouring seats. As I passed in front of this café I heard these rude recitatives, scattered as the sounds of an orchestra tuning, and their conversation meant no more to me than an echo of their songs. These men were for me the first foreigners, those whose language I could not understand, at a time when I was beginning to distinguish the different Arab dialects: those of the Jews, Moslems and Christians. Later, as an adolescent, I recognised the half-forgotten faces of these porters in the features of my history and civics teacher. The government obliged the Jewish school I attended to have Moslem teachers in those subjects where orthodoxy was essential: history, civics, geography. Our teacher was a Kurd and his accent made him vulnerable to our sarcasm. One day, driven to despair by our bad behaviour, he sadly expressed his admiration for our intelligence and his regret at our blindness. Could we not see that he was on our side, that he did not want to impose anything upon us? His appeal, yet another mark of weakness in our eyes, made him seem all the more ridiculous to us, pitifully funny.

I often passed in front of the Kurdish café. I never stopped, and it would have seemed to me absurd to go in.

82

Not from lack of curiosity, but because I would have felt that I was breaking an unwritten law, infringing on an intimacy that no formal barriers protected, apart from a tacit agreement between Kurds and Arabs. The territory of the Other is sacred, provided the borders are recognised. If they are not, of course, blood will flow.

On first sight nothing distinguished us, the Jews, from Moslems or Christians. There was no ghetto, though we tended to live near the synagogues. Yet we were easily singled out: by our dialect, our dress, sometimes even our features. The same applied to the Christians. They too had their distinctive vocabulary, their characteristic accent. No one tried to deny his own community, for who could imagine its non-existence? We knew that among themselves the Moslems recognised each other specifically as Shiites or Sunnites, and among these the tribal affiliation identified people from a given region, even from towns. These identities are not mere extensions of desert life. They have a past, a secular heritage. I learned in school that Baghdad was planned and built by an Abbasid caliph. Moslems, Christians or Jews, Arabs or Kurds, we were not all descendants of the Bedouins. For us the city was at once our common fortress and our particular village. But we knew that this fortress, built on the shores of two rivers, was surrounded with sand and had been stolen from the desert.

The sheik is not lord of a territory. He has no fortified seat. His domain is a region which he maintains against rival tribes. He is the sage, the elder, the guide who leads a group of men in a common action. His only resource is his honour, which he must constantly defend in order to preserve his authority. The group of which he is chief is a community based not on the will to devastate and dominate nature, to exploit its resources and enjoy its benefits, but on the will to defend itself against nature's rigours. This nature is not an ally in the struggle to preserve and develop life: it is the menace, the enemy.

Islam has been able in the past to unite scattered wills and give them a reason for being, a means of surpassing themselves; not to console them for the rigours of their fate but to teach them to be masters of it. It was not land they had to occupy, but history; or, rather, the conquest of territory was only a means in that march toward the inscription of a group of men in history, in the name of an absolute guided by a supreme force. As history itself was subject to God, the domination of history was the accomplishment of His will. Men relied on the higher force to become masters of a hostile land, and their relations with each other were direct and precise. Submissive to God, distinguished one from the other only by the quality of their piety, they were united in a common movement whose meaning and ultimate purpose was beyond their understanding. The group had its own intrinsic qualities. It needed no sense of territorial belonging, no mythic dramatisation, to become fact and be aware of its own existence. Its strength and resources came from within itself. It defined itself neither by its possessions nor by a birthplace, but by the deeds of its ancestors, the quality of its leaders, and its own solid unity.

The conquest of history ended in the founding of an empire which went through the stages common to all temporal enterprises: dynamism, maturity and decadence. But the group persisted. It was no longer armed with transcendency and could no longer cover its actions by declarations of submission to a superior will. Defeat and failure robbed the movement of meaning and direction. The group had only its own resources with which to perpetuate itself, and was obliged, if it were not to dissolve, to preserve its identity by preventing any change in the features that distinguished and characterised it. What had been a bond for carrying out great actions became a wall to protect the existence of those features. Thus one is known in the desert by the tribe one belongs to, and in the city by one's speech or religion.

In Baghdad the Jews lived around the synagogues, the Christians clustered around their churches, and the Moslems were everywhere. There were no ghettos, and while the Jews differed from the Moslems in their headdress, the Shiites also dressed differently from the Sunnites. What struck me as an anomaly and fascinated me at the same time was the variety of dialects within the city. All of us, Moslems, Jews and Christians, spoke Arabic, and we had all chosen to speak it differently. In the case of the Jews, if it had simply been a matter of embellishing their speech with Hebraic terms — and they all knew the language of prayer — there would have been nothing surprising about it. But they, like the other groups, had their own pronunciation and their own way of changing the words of the classic language, so that each group traced the borders of its collective view of life and affirmed its will to determine in its own way the nature of relationships between man and man.

If the tribe, by pronouncing its name, announces its will and desire to dominate nature, the religious community is the sign of a distinctive group life born of a common search for a relationship with the beyond. This initial purpose is perpetuated in action and in the collective life of the group. It creates common interests and draws lines of defence for the group's protection. Each group displays its sign through the word. Dialect is not a wall to protect against the hostile gaze of others, but a fence to warn them to respect an intimate fact. In the desert each tribe knows the needs and dangers of other tribes. In the city, where each group came into existence by virtue of its members' relationship with the beyond, the varied privacies grow hostile to each other only when one group begins to defend its community life rather than its relationship with the beyond. Then it clashes with other groups. The Moslems respect the religions of the Jews and Christians, for they mark the frontiers of the privacy of others. Collective jealousies and frustrations are directed at Jews and Christians only as social groups with material interests to defend and protect. The neighbour's privacy is respected out of fear that one's own may be violated. The neighbour's relationship with God, even if it is direct, becomes for us theatrical because it is foreign to our own. And even if our respect for the neighbour is real and spontaneous the foreignness of his relationship to God makes him less real, and his life becomes a spectacle for us. The privacy that cannot be shared inevitably turns into a theatre for others. It is sacred for us, and the respect we accord it is as natural to us as our indifference to the Other's religion. It would never have occurred to a Moslem to convert a Jew or a Christian. Their religion is theatre for him and hence unreal. There is no point in opposing it, for it is competition only for other unrealities. For the possessors of reality it is no more than spectacle: trivial entertainment. Reality is the religion that one lives.

———————

The Ottomans tried to pursue the Islamic enterprise of the Arabs. They were mere instruments of continuity, not true heirs to the message that came from the desert. Once the relationship with the desert had been lost, nothing remained of the original mission of Islam but the continuation of a process. An efficient continuation, to be sure, which both proved itself and knew its times of decadence.

The Arabs tried to integrate Spain into history by establishing the reign of Islam. The Ottomans had no such ambitions. In Hungary they built minarets where there had been Christian cupolas, but this was to proclaim the presence of an Empire for which Islam was only a mechanism of sovereignty and an instrument of power. When the states of Europe, at the height of their dynamism, forced the *Sick Man* to give autonomy to Christian minorities, the *millet,* or religious community, was institutionalised. Arab Islam had always recognised the particular group existences of the Peoples of the Book. The Ottoman sultans turned this recognition into a political system, one that the British were later to adopt and pursue, spontaneously and without reservations, in Egypt.

During the last years of the war the British, whose forces were occupying the country, installed a cultural institute in Baghdad, the British Council, where Iraqi citizens (who had demonstrated their hostility to Great Britain in 1941) could take English lessons and listen to speakers and piano recitals. The same group always turned up there. Most of us were Jewish, some were Christians and a very few were Moslems. Great Britain showed herself to us in all her majesty, munificence and democracy. We were let in on the secret of her power. Occasionally we met a few natives of those distant isles, but mostly they kept to themselves. I had a vague intuition that the efforts of the British were not intended to make us admire them, still less to make us love them. They were to show them to us as they were, to reveal their true face, unmasked. At the time I was convinced we would finally recognise that they were not our enemies but our allies. It was not a question of being friends but of facing facts. There they were, on our soil, and we might as well accept their presence and collaborate with them.

Lectures on the blessings of British institutions did not try to present these as examples to be followed. With no vanity (but with much pride) they revealed the secrets of supremacy. All they asked was that we bow to the accomplished fact. But this civilisation that was held up for our wonderment was not our own and never would be. It was autonomous and self-sufficient, but not exportable. We were foreigners and nothing could be done to admit us to such an admirable life-discipline. This Occident would always send me back to my origins, would never be my liberator. Indifferent, it relegated me to the Orient of my birth, an Orient by now transformed for me into spectacle.

It was through books that I discovered the French Occident. This was something quite different from my heart-breaking acquaintance with snippets of British civilisation, which implacably sent me back — though now as an alien — to my own sources. France seemed to me the sole repository and clue to the one and veritable Occident. French was my first lesson in enchantment. I could knock at Europe's door; I would be let in. I had only to recognise its universality. This culture of France was a summons to mankind. There was one origin and one species: it was universal, but universality had its own language, and its voice was French. I had no need to verify what for me represented an eloquent message designed for all mankind. But what if the French themselves were not worthy ambassadors of the message? On the other hand, what did it matter, so long as they invited me to this exacting celebration of humanity? My faith could equal theirs. My encounter with the French surpassed all my expectations. From the moment I arrived, Paris appeared to me not as a reality that one singles out routinely among the crowd of ambiguities and contradictions, but as a luminous truth that is thrust upon the mind, calling on every resource of sensitivity, stilling all resistance.

This city stands like a dogma to which one submits by an act of faith. And one never exhausts the possibilities of a dogma one has not rejected. I *learned* the city, as we learn a lesson that transforms us and modifies our vision. It was only much later, in foreign America, that I could puzzle out the contours of a reality into which I had plunged, losing myself, a reality that from then on became my own. Paradoxically this city, born of a colossal abstraction, can be possessed only through love. And it is not detachment that lets us perceive reality, but involvement. For Paris is the masterpiece and grandiose symbol of what the French call universality, which is merely their way of establishing a rapport with reality. For centuries the French have embellished and refined the translation into concrete terms of a majestic theorem. The point of departure is not man. He deserves the grandeur and profusion of nature only if he succeeds in superimposing his truth on hers. And if the task appears impossible it is because man lacks energy, is not worthy of his own truth. But if man's truth exists, if he creates it and imposes it on the truth of nature, his rapport with reality is not a direct one. It must pass through the mediation of dogma. Paris bears witness to this kind of apprehension of reality. There is a beauty which exists exterior to man. It consists of harmony, orchestrated according to a geometry that is satisfying to all the senses. It is clear, precise and comprehensible. Paris shines like a picture in which everything has been foreseen, where nothing is left to chance, where folly itself contributes to order, for it is a reminder of the terror in which there is no order. If we walk through Paris with an open mind we cannot avoid the certainty that the project of an exemplary city antedates the memory of man, who has been intent on building it through all his centuries. This is his answer to the abundance of nature. He manufactures a second nature to affirm his own presence, a nature which is an extension of himself. Here he acquires his right to privacy, privacy with himself or rather with the image of himself which, knowingly and arbitrarily, he projects. Thus he avoids all direct relations with nature, and his relations with the group are filtered through an abstraction of himself, a reflection of man in general and of his exemplary prototype, the Frenchman. Thus Paris is not the product of the will of the Parisians. They are the product of their city. It is their home. They do not live in a house, but in an entire city. And the whole majestic project is the preserve of foreigners, tourists and provincials, who choose to find themselves by losing themselves within it. And the others? In every street, in every city block Parisians carve out a village made to their own measure, and answer the call to surpass themselves only in great and exceptional circumstances.

———————————

London is not easily grasped as one strolls through its streets. It is a city that remains foreign to me, for I see only the separate, discordant elements. The common design escapes me. I have often been told: the city must be conquered with patience; it will finally reach through to you and win you over. But what struck me was its foreignness. The little houses, the streets, the sections of the town forming little villages. Here men gathered one by one, of their own free will, to form a mass. Every Londoner is a citizen enjoying inalienable rights as an individual, and the city was born of agreement and compromise among a multitude of individuals. Liberty is not a universal given, an abstraction; it attaches to persons, individuals who are alone before nature. The Londoner has no direct relationship with nature, any more than does the Parisian. He too sets up in opposition to it a second nature, constructed in this case by a group of abstractions called individuals. Each one sees himself through the image projected for him of his liberty, his power, his relationships with nature and with others. He is left to himself and to the discomfort he cannot dispel (except by the prolongation of the abstraction of which he is, despite himself, the expression), in a world where he is a stranger and alone. Confronted by a nature that is separate and distinct he constructs a world in his image, makes laws and institutions that regulate and protect the liberties of the individual. But this abstraction, even if it is laminated to the concrete and itself appears to be concrete, is nonetheless superimposed.

London and Paris, exemplary cities. They illustrate the inability of western man to insert himself into nature. By opposite paths Parisians and Londoners construct their distinct theatres as substitutes for what is out of their reach: life within a nature that is real. These city-theatres, final achievements of a civilisation, govern the relationships of man with his neighbour.

For a long time I wrote off as another contradiction of life the fact that the French, with their thirst for the universal, have so little understanding for all those who fail to recognise that universality must have the features and form of France — sole rescuer of the universal from the state of limbo. A corollary contradiction is the indifference of the English, so concerned with the liberties of the individual, to the liberty of those who are not of the communion of institutions of some part of the British Isles. For those not born under the flag of the Republic — those who are not sons of the Revolution — the French admit only one means of emancipation: an act of conversion and an oath of fidelity to the principles of the Republic and the Revolution. If one is not born French one can become French. Liberty and equality begin in France.

––––––––––––––––––

The British soldiers I met in Baghdad despised those Iraqis who adopted British customs and traditions, which are, of course, not exportable. They had spent centuries perfecting a game which makes society forget that it is only theatre and people forget that they are merely shadows. The game-board does not travel well. And the English cannot bear to watch a masquerade that exposes the fragility of their certainties and the absence of rapport between the English and their neighbours in the world. They do not wish to be shown a caricature of themselves. Thus, in different ways, the French and English deny the group, because the civilisations they have built were created in the absence of a direct rapport between man and his neighbour.

For an Englishman all men are foreigners, and all foreigners are to be mistrusted—and annihilated by contempt. For the foreigner, who does not have an abstract image of himself as a free individual, casts doubt upon the whole abstraction. The man who lives constantly within theatricality can have no rapport with others unless there is a theatre to mediate that rapport. What terrifies the English most in Arab countries is the native's habit of touching those with whom he speaks. Touching invades the autonomy of the individual;

91

it obliges him to lose himself and find himself again in rapport with others. This negation of the group, which is a negation of the Other, has marked all of Britain's history.

The Magna Carta deprived the King of his pretended authority to proclaim a collective policy for the country. Each lord set up a restricted project of his own. Already the model that gave birth to London can be seen taking form. And the English adopted Protestantism because it corresponded to choices already made, to the kind of relationship they had established with reality. The point of departure is not a collective theatre in which each individual sees himself and accepts his place, but an individual theatre which, when multiplied, is the substance of a collective theatre no less restrictive, no less capable of becoming oppressive when opposed. The English accepted the creation of collective theatres by the Scots, the Welsh and the Irish, out of the anarchy of individuals; but they rejected any attempt to pursue a line other than the one that had resulted in British institutions. After a long struggle the Scots finally adopted the institutions and religion of the English; but having recognised their defeat they took off to conquer the strongholds of the Empire: its banks, its colonies, its political life. They ended up ruling Great Britain. The Irish reacted otherwise. Their religion became their armour, their territory a fortress to protect their difference, which they defended with their blood. While the Scots turned their defeat into victory, the victory of the Irish plunged them into a long distress. In fact, when one theatre enters into conflict with another, neither wins. Is the bitter determination with which a particular theatre is defended the sign of a struggle toward a full life in which man will no longer veil from himself the light of reality? Or is it the harrowing, raucous cry of impotent anger, the pain of despair? This bitterness struck with the greatest cruelty and savagery against those colonies most opposed to having their rapport with reality governed by a theatrical power that tended to make a spectacle of all reality outside its own theatre. While the British coloniser imposed his power he allowed the native to manage his own family and maintain his traditions and customs, for these did not threaten the fragility of the second reality by which the master lived. On the contrary, they helped him to forget that fragility. The exotic has always helped the English forget their anxieties. In their times of greatest malaise it has provided them with entertainment. But to be capable of being transformed into a spectacle, the native must remain different. He is assigned his theatricality, and it does not even serve to mediate an evanescent reality. He is spectacle pure and simple, there to reassure and console his masters.

In the wake of the soldiers and police, the guardians of British culture lent a strong hand to the vicious and frightened attempt to extinguish all trace of a present Orient from the West, along with the faintest vestiges of a primal Orient. The assassination took many forms, sometimes subtle, or veiled by an apparent good-will that deceived even itself. A new science was created: Oriental Studies. For earnest undergraduates this mass of humanity, this East teeming with life, was buried under scrupulous research into semantics, historical events and theological subtleties. Orientalism, by seizing on the vitality of the Orient, reduced it to a dead form: a theatre. Puritans eager for escape sought in the distant desert to lose their unhappiness. Kipling was a contemporary of Doughty, and T. E. Lawrence of Fitzgerald.

The French style of Orientalism is quite different, though it ends in a similar swindle. Massignon devoted his life to the study of Arab literature and the Islamic religion. But for him Al Hallaj was no more than a mediator who ensured that Massignon's conversion to Catholicism should be accomplished in exaltation. Even his broad-minded appeal for unity among the Abrahamic religions was perhaps no more than the search for an abstraction, a universal dogma. This search for things in common is in the final analysis merely a refusal to accept differences. All things converged toward the final verity of Catholicism which, by extension, was perhaps a French verity as well. The struggle for sameness and conformity was the basis of French civilisation. In the King's name, and later in the name of the Republic, the cultures of Brittany, Languedoc and Provence were reduced to the status of folklore. With a mixture of nostalgia and rage some French provincials (the word is a clue to their status) try to save their secular cultures from oblivion. But it is shameful to resist French universality; to oppose it actively is a heinous sin. This universality maintained its identical dogmatic base even when its content changed with times and circumstances: first monarchical and Catholic, then secular and revolutionary, but always totalitarian. This is why any change it undergoes must be a total overthrow brought about by violence.

It is not easy to convert those who believe in a dramaturgy, particularly if the alternative offered them is merely another kind of theatre. Secular education in France has not eliminated a parallel school system operated by the Church. The die-hards of the Old Regime fought a long, losing battle against the Republicans. Each group claimed to represent France and its universality; each had its own France in mind. Believers in a tattered past ranged themselves against what they considered a travesty of the real France.

The French exported France to their colonies, or at least what they thought was France. They imposed not laws and institutions on the natives, but ideals. Of course there was a gap between the principles of liberty, equality and fraternity as applied to the soldiers and functionaries of the Republic, and the treatment they inflicted on those they governed. But this was not an insuperable contradiction. Equality was for the French. Yet their superiority was not a privilege of birth; it was a quality that could be acquired through an act of faith and practised through conviction. Any native could raise himself to the status of French equality. He need only be worthy of the fraternity offered him. His liberty was the liberty to become French. Thus it is

94

quite normal to hear black Africans repeating the history lesson that has been drilled into them: "Our ancestors, the Gauls . . ."

Parallel to the Arab courses prescribed by the Iraqi government, we prepared for the French *certificat d'études,* or elementary school finals, at the School of the Universal Israelite Alliance of Baghdad. We learned the geography of France in minute detail. What was our joy to find our own Mesopotamia, at last, hidden in the vastness of Asia! We covered it in four sentences. Obviously, the native is not utterly condemned to the condition of being a foreigner. He can become French if he pays the price. But it is not quite enough that he be converted to the faith of his masters: he must also know how to practise their faith. For that matter, the same price is paid by every metropolitan Frenchman, but the native, whether black, yellow or white, loses a few more feathers in the process. If he agrees to leave behind his own past, to accept a theatre instead of reality, he gains access to French universality and in the end sees himself as the French see him: the involuntary product of a civilisation dead or condemned to disappear on contact with French universality. And in the schism of his being, in the confusion of theatre and reality, he annihilates himself and begins to despise his own past. If he is rich enough or flexible enough he achieves the metamorphosis, or else he rebels, refusing to disappear even if he is offered the temptation of rebirth in a materially higher form. If his rapport with reality is highly enough developed, if he has not already been won over by the theatrical, he will reject a process that reduces him to an odd vestige of the past, an exotic and amusing specimen. Those whom France has shaped, their minds moulded by her spirit, rise up in revolt. Yet they cannot use against her an old way of life that is helpless before her irresistible theatre. In the end they adopt her system, and oppose her theatre with a new one of their own. We have seen the birth of a whole series of centrifugal abstractions that take a variety of names according to circumstances. In Africa the name may be negritude, communocracy or socialism. In Algeria, Arabism. In Asia, communism.

France gauges the degree of development of a people by its readiness to assimilate French universality. Thus, despite its backwardness and its inclusion in Islam, Algeria could be treated as French territory. Helping factors, to be sure, were the presence of a strong Francophone minority and the fragility of Algeria's Arabism. The Algerian war took on its particular bitterness because it challenged the centripetal force, the power of attraction and the civilising superiority of French universality.

How could a people prefer its medieval state when it could have freedom, progress and the privilege of belonging to the up-and-coming fraction of humanity? Unless, of course, some mental aberration or external and malevolent forces were at play... The French and British both attempted, after the fall of their empires, to maintain their presence, in a variety of more or less substantial forms, in their ex-colonies. France gave a new name to its concept of universality: *la francophonie.* Great Britain, retreating from its former territories, tried to maintain a gossamer hold upon them within the Commonwealth, a motley assembly with no pretentions to effectiveness.

Relationships with God could have filled the void left in the West by the absence of the group. But Catholicism and Protestantism merely shored up two forms of theatre. Catholic dogma was parallel to the dogma of monarchy, and gave it, within a temporal theatre that ensured its domination, divine backing if not an outright guarantee. The relationship with God could not in these circumstances weld together a community by linking it directly to the forces of the beyond. But religion did supply, to a collection of men subordinated to a common abstraction (though in a way that did not consolidate them into a group), a second abstraction which dulled their desire for a direct rapport with God by the action of intercessors and mediators.

The Revolution in its violence revived the authority of the mediators while giving them a new vocabulary. The God that united men was no longer in the beyond. He was among the men who, in the bloody name of the Revolution, forged new relationships which were quite as indirect as the old, even when they were the fruit of sacrifice. Men did not see each other more clearly than before, in their particularity. They had a new dogma to believe in. Their commitment was no longer to a king, and their obedience did not spring from a sense of belonging to a territory. Enter: a new abstraction called the "nation." At a time when religion could no longer survive the new centrifugal forces of the cities, where people identified themselves only as residents of one part of town, the rapport with nature had grown as agonisingly unreal as that between man and his neighbour. In the city, the earth could no longer live up to that ancient illusion, the old image of the nursing mother. It seemed to have been pushed away, exiled by the machine which piled men together in such a way that they could no longer see or recognise each other, no longer establish any real rapport. The nation makes it possible to link man with his neighbour through the mediation of a theatre that dispenses with God. This new abstraction emptied individuals of their specific content by melting them together with a multitude of other individualities. What was more, the nation replaced the homeland. What had been a rapport with nature (whether hostile, domesticated or dominated) became an attachment to an abstraction with pretensions to including, in one vast totality, nature, the individual and the group. For the French the nation could represent a reality because it seemed to provide a moral, para-religious base, an indispensable tool for the implantation of power: it justified conquest. French universality thus extended its abstraction to others and pretended to liberate them, while in fact subduing them.

It is understandable that the English had no need for this abstraction, since their form of theatre contradicts the dogma of universality (even if, in its final form, it coincides with it). It was Britain's institutions and their supremacy that gave the Empire its justification and its base.

It was in another country (where the nation had no empire or theatre to give it the basis for becoming a great power) that the idea of the nation became the subject of philosophical and ideological reflections, dark, subtle and interminable.

A domain of this world would have given German theatre a semblance of reality, but Germany did not have such domain. Whence its ever more frenzied, more anguished search for a rapport with reality. The theatre-nation was impotent to mediate. And the Nazi blood-bath was the dead-end of the process — an attempt to give justifying substance to a theatre which was, in any case, dedicated to exacerbating the absence of any authentic relation to what is real. Nazism was the extreme case of western theatricality: a folklore without a folk.

A few years ago I took part in a world congress of journalism in Cairo. Official receptions, a press conference with President Nasser, excursions. . . . The President invited us to an evening in the Nile-Hilton hotel, where the attraction was a dance show. In this hotel the waiters wore the livery of an imaginary Orient, half-Turkish, half-Arab. No doubt Hollywood had had its say in this stylisation. On the stage it was pushed even further. Arab dancing, when the complicity between dancers and spectators is lost, is no longer sensual and erotic but vulgar and obscene. Eroticism turns to sexual mimicry and dancers and spectators become sellers and buyers of merchandise. The guardians of public morality in the Nasser regime did not want completely to forbid the dance that had made their country famous. They applied

98

themselves to bowdlerising its explosive qualities. What had been a ceremony became a spectacle in which the public, unable to participate, experienced only the surprise of the exotic. Bellies are covered, thighs exposed. This dance, evolved for the palace, took on the aspect of a folk-dance choreographed by an American film director. I expressed my surprise to our Egyptian hosts. They found me very out-of-date. It was obvious to them that their stylisation was a great step forward from the dance one saw in cabarets before Nasser's revolution. An Algerian delegate exclaimed that even in this improved form the belly-dance would remain forbidden in his country, because it degraded woman-hood. Our Egyptian friend, on the other hand, was convinced that this style of dancing, thanks to the modifications brought about, had won itself a place in the civilised world of show-business. Full-circle. The way had been long, filled with obstacles and rejections, but finally the West had won. Hollywood adapts a few elements of the traditional Orient to stir the fizzling senses of spectators wide-eyed before a cardboard exoticism. What theatre could be more elementary? This cheap westernisation seems to the Eastern mind to be the first step in its ascent to civilisation. The theatre on which such minds thrive is not even of their own creation, but a tawdry second-hand article.

There is nothing sudden about these developments. They are the result of a process that began at the end of the nineteenth century. The pioneers and ideological fathers of Arab nationalism, Al-Afghani and Abdou particularly, discovered in Europe the explosive possibilities of drama-tising the collectivity. They realised that what gave western power its moral and spiritual armament, and what justified that power in the eyes of those who exercised it, was the theatrical extension of the individual in an abstract collec-tivity, imaginary and dramatised. Perhaps without full aware-ness of what he was doing Al-Afghani conceived a strategy of defence for the Arab, or rather the Eastern, world (he himself was not of Arab descent). The strategy was counter-attack. In

99

his eyes the West was trying to break down the remaining cohesion in the East, its relationship to reality, to inflict a defeat more final than the one already achieved by western armies. To repulse this moral attack it was necessary to forge a spiritual and moral framework for the Orient modelled on that of the West. Thus the foundation for Arab nationalism was laid. Al-Afghani quickly saw that the secular nation could have no meaning for cities separated by desert, and still less for the Bedouins who lived in the desert. Only Islam could hold together these scattered elements with orders that were simple, clear, precise and binding. The fact that Al-Afghani himself was not a believer was not for him a serious obstacle, for he saw in religion not a relationship with God that governed relations between men, but a dramatisation essentially political in nature. As a result his worst enemies were not the English and the French but the Ottomans. The latter, Moslems themselves, were no longer capable of manipulating in western style the political force which religion represented. They were, to be sure, perverting the original vocation of Islam, but their way of exploiting it seemed more and more anachronistic. For Al-Afghani, as for all the eastern nationalists of the period, the West was an ally against this decrepit enemy, the *sick man*, this Orient crumbling irrevocably into its own ruins.

The Iraqi poet Maaruf al Rassafi was an anti-Ottoman nationalist. And the meeting of T. E. Lawrence with the masters of the desert was as much sought after by them as by himself. For the shereef Hussein this blond soldier possessed the secret of western magic and could pass it to an Orient attempting to leave its past behind. For Lawrence, on the other hand, the Bedouins held a secret much more precious than any the West had ever possessed: rapport with reality. But Lawrence did not realise that they despised what to him seemed a priceless and irreplaceable gift. The misunderstanding between Lawrence and the Bedouins was total. As a poet he found in their reality something that surpassed poetry. For the politicians he was only a tool. The price he had to pay for accomplishing his voyage into the land of reality was an exorbitant one. It finally cost him his life.

At the end of the first world war the Arabs had little understanding that those who had given them the means to their liberation were now installed in their lands as the new masters. Guided by the French and English, they had made their entry into the world of dramatisation and intended to become masters of their theatre, even if it was a borrowed one. Their confrontation with the West obliged them to model their theatre even more obviously on that of their new masters (or those who hoped to be their masters). The champions of Islam set up a bitter resistance to the West, rejecting it completely, but the Islamic religion could hardly be interpreted according to Western criteria. The Moslems, out of phase with an industrial century, could not re-create the rapport of desert man with reality. They were led to dramatise their relationships with men, and reduce their faith to an instrument of political and social action. An anachronism, they became a store-front sect. Despite themselves they wore a mask, and the mask belonged to a reality that had disappeared.

Gradually pan-Islamism gave way to pan-Arabism. The political history of the Middle East after Al Nahda (the rebirth) is the history of attempts to assimilate western ideologies and political systems. In Iraq the English installed an administration modelled on that of London. Letter-boxes have the same shape and colour in Baghdad and Liverpool. Ministers are elected and responsible to Parliament. To ensure that this tradition took root without too much risk for British nationals, and that the mechanism set in motion functioned in the interest of the occupiers, London (whose armed forces were entrenched in two bases closed to natives) put British advisers in high posts in the Iraqi administration. The minister signed; the adviser decided.

The French proceded differently in Lebanon. They administered the country directly, and when they finally recognized its autonomy they put in decisive positions local converts to French universality. French culture was not, for that matter, considered as something entirely foreign. A large section of the population of Lebanon is Christian by long tradition and Christianity is at home there. Lebanese Christians had long ago chosen universality. It is surprising to note that there is no fissure between Arab and French cultures in this country, and that there have even been writers who — a risky business — worked within both cultures (Said Akl for example). The fact is that French universality did not condemn the Lebanese to being eternal natives, and did not reduce them to the status of perpetual foreigners in relation to the West.

In Egypt the British presence did not prevent the elite of that country (probably because of the large number of Lebanese immigrants) from making French universality their own and attaching themselves to the West via France.

The discovery of the West was not accompanied by effective domestic measures. The past had to be doctored to bring it in tune with the welcome being given the West. Even then, the ideological tools the West provided were only usable in a western framework, and this framework attracted the new oriental elites, who sought power for themselves rather than a reformed vision of the world or a rediscovery of authentic rapport with reality. For the western theatre to be at all effective a fictional reality had to be created. Parliamentary governments and institutions were set up to justify the ideological apparatus that would allow the eastern elite to assume or demand its place in the system. Western parliamentary government seemed like a ritual with no roots in past or present, a game from which the dramatic element was eliminated, or simply a straightforward entertainment, which did not, however, see itself as such. To a new elite produced by the universities and the army, the system seemed likely to bring them to power and, above all, to keep them there. The army was an instrument of brute efficiency which, in the absence of any ideology, was justified solely by the fact of its existence. For such an elite nationalism is an ideal instrument. It harks back to a refurbished past to justify an artificial present. That present buries reality under an ideology whose sole purpose is to arouse emotion and give it an outlet. From this moment on the East has its theatre in the form of Arab nationalism. The British were so aware of this fiction and its effectiveness that they tried to exploit it for their own benefit. They were the instigators of the Arab League.

A political ideology can endure if it gives dramatic coherence to a political power. Changes in ideology are merely an indication of a change in the theatrical base of the political system. This explains the vague, ephemeral and shifting character of ideological dramatisations when they do not reflect the reality of political power. Nazism, in its moment of triumph, attracted young Arab intellectuals and officers. Its collapse in Europe was followed by its immediate disappearance from the Arab horizon. A West that is not effective cannot serve as model. To counteract the power of France and Britain, the East always looked west for instruments of combat and dramatic coherence. It was not surprising after the war that former admirers of Hitler became disciples of Stalin.

But then the Arab countries were left to themselves with theatrical machinery which they did not control. The heirs of Stalin were no longer the distant, glorious creators of a reassuring theatre, but the representatives of an established power which, whatever its ideology, could supply arms and munitions. The dramatisation of Arabism did not result in Arab unity. Monarchs and military dictators defended the restricted interests of a region or country, each draped in the cast-offs of fidelity to the Arab cause, each heaping anathema on all the others as traitors to that cause. The ideological dramatisations each sovereign used to legitimize his power were so vague and flimsy that no political regime could be sure of a long life.

Walking in the streets of Cairo and Alexandria a few years ago I was assailed by the sight of endless banderoles whose message, monotonous as a recitative, sang the blessings of socialism. Repetition was used with the same force that gives the inscriptions of verses from the Koran in public places their ritual necessity. But the political slogans set a scene on which no human being appeared, either as actor or spectator. The words were merely words, with nothing behind them.

Arab politicians in office make use of western ideological terms, either to up-date an old style of rhetoric or to confound their adversaries (which does not prevent them from throwing the latter in prison as well, or having them assassinated). The use of this foreign terminology is an amusing spectator game for amateurs in dialectics, but a confusing one for western journalists to follow if they attempt a systematic analysis of political speeches and editorials from the Arab world. Of course the heavy mask of ideological theatre sometimes reveals glimpses of the existence of clans, friendships, tribal attachments and religious loyalties. A dramaturgy is not altered by a simple change of decor. What the Arabs most bitterly resent in Israel is its apparent ability to assimilate western dramaturgy and feel at ease within it, even using it as a defence. Appearances may justify Arab resentment, but it is a fact that Israel cannot accept the West without a serious loss. In Israel, where people do not easily give up the Orient, there are many who have eastern roots and many others who have not forgotten that, in a hostile Europe, Judaism stood for a primal Orient whose vision, despite its failure, is indestructible. With the arrival in Israel of western elements, contempt also makes its appearance. The Yemenites, the Moroccan and Kurdish Jews must be civilised. Along with mathematics and physics they must be taught Polish cooking so as to liberate them from the burden of eastern primitivism. The more Israel affirms its western character the more discomfort it will experience. More than by conflicts of interest, Israel and the Arab countries are divided by their different ways of

104

scuttling reality and welcoming the West as it bears its dramaturgies.

The American revolution began with a tea-party, a symbol that coincides with the real reasons for the confrontation of the Anglo-Saxon immigrants and the mother-country. When they landed in the New World, the "pilgrims" had no intention of disavowing the theatre on which the Empire was built. If they sinned it was through excessive orthodoxy. They were radicals who accused the Empire of outliving its own theatre. These puritans wanted to rediscover in its original purity the dramatisation by which they lived. The Dominon of God affirms the supremacy of the individual, giving him the means to stage-manage his relations with God without being disturbed by reality, always a menace to purity and inconveniently ambiguous. But the pilgrims arrived in a ready-made decor that was not of their choice. This rich and abundant nature had not been in their plans. It seemed to them the ally of instinct, and instinct was the enemy. Nature must be dominated, devastated if need be, to throttle its living force. But in the name of what unifying dramatisation? The monarchy? The Empire? Was the Dominion to be no more than a prolongation of what was already established in London? An impossible contradiction. In this new decor the old theatre could no longer mediate between man and nature, nor, as a result, between man and his neighbour. The freedom to devastate nature, to occupy a continent and dig out its riches, gave to a host of pilgrims, adventurers without a cause, the sense of a possible community. The fact that their bond was not a direct rapport with reality but the search for a new dramatisation was of no importance. The first obstacle was the old, inadequate dramatisation, which provided them neither with instruments for devastating nature nor with the means to establish a real relationship with it. And so a new theatre was born in North America.

105

In it the adventurers found their cause; they became Americans, building their theatre on a double dramatisation, that of the British individual and that of French universality. In the new democracy everyone was given the same rights and had the same freedom to devastate nature. But some cohesion had to be given this multitude in its struggle with a savage nature. The first step was to consider the original occupants of the territory as elements of nature. These savages deserved no better treatment than the nature which sheltered them. They could be decimated with a clear conscience.

The new occupiers closed ranks. All amusement was seen as the work of the devil, or an alliance with nature, or an undermining of the theatre which, from the moment of its creation, became all-powerful. A rigorous law reigned over morals. It had to be all the more rigorous because the hostile landscape created stresses that begged for relaxation. The double dramatisation continued, making more acute the basic contradiction of American theatricality: on the one hand, a personal theatre, of which the individual is master, allowed each man to develop his particular adventure to its extreme. On the other hand a collective theatre imprisoned him and forced him to give up at least part of the pattern of his individuality. The collision took place when the *group* (ethnic, religious or regional) broke open both the sovereignty of the individual theatre and the cohesion of the collective theatre. Each generation of Americans produced a rallying-point to melt its groups into a common dramatisation, whether it was called the melting-pot or integration or cultural pluralism. Yet the groups formed despite these attempts at collective dramatisations. The theory is that each individual is master of his theatre, yet the white Protestant lives the dramatisation of his American life differently from the Irish Catholic, and the Italian Catholic has a form of theatre that differs from that of the Jew. Those who have noticed, consciously or unconsciously, the basic contradiction of this double dramatisation, have tried to find points of intersection, some harmony in the whole. For this to be possible the collective promises would have had to be fulfilled on the individual level: the Italian should have had an equal chance with the Anglo-Saxon Protestant.

The case of the Black cannot be compared with these different levels of assimilation. He was imported as an implement and reduced to an element of nature. As a slave he carried out his orders to devastate nature. But once freed and endowed with a will he constituted an adverse element: not an ally of man against nature but a weapon that nature sharpens against her own destroyers. Every time the Black affirms his freedom he is pointed at as a malevolent force; he is singled out as a resurgence of blind instinct, and is feared because he bears on his face the marks of his dangerous origins. Though the Anglo-Saxon jealously guards his own birthright, the collective theatre allows isolated individuals to be accepted as members of the privileged group; but only on certain conditions, such as changing names or switching religions. Thus the Jew Goldwasser becomes the Protestant Goldwater. Those who remain attached to their group must wait their turn. When the Kennedys come on the scene the exclusivity is relaxed a little. The Irish have made it. The process is irreversible, even if vice-presidential candidates have to be called Agnew and Muskie to conceal their Greek and Polish origins. Does their acceptance mean a promotion for the entire group from which they come, or the acceptance of that group by the majority? If so this would mean not only a total upset of the hegemony of one group or a partial loss of its privileges, but also a questioning of its theatre, if not its complete disappearance. Let us imagine a Greek immigrant who insists on his origin, not because he needs reassurance (all the while declaring that it now means nothing to him), but because he has no need to deny it: it is quietly and surreptitiously disappearing into a dream of the past. The pride we hear in his declaration of origin is a formality, for his fidelity has no object, is empty, theatrical. Is there such a thing as an ethnic group which is not threatened by its own folklore and ostentatious loyalty to its past? This would indeed be the overthrow of a whole civilisation, and would certainly not pass unnoticed.

If the individual no longer feels the need to link himself to reality through a collective or individual theatre, it means that he has established a direct rapport with that reality, and can give birth to a true community. The group will no longer be ethnic, religious or regional, but human. Its characteristics will be the result of a tacit consent. In this sense a community is a group of men who undertake to live collectively without the intermediary of theatre. We are far from this stage, but the need for it is felt and present. Some can afford the luxury — for it is a luxury reserved for the rich to create a community of this kind artificially. At the other end of the economic scale the hippies and yippies are easily turned into mountebanks by the hostile or mocking majority of those who see them, and the community they have voluntarily constituted becomes a spectacle. They are cornered in a minority position and the futility of their protest reduces them to a collection of marginal oddities. They cannot overthrow an established order of dramatisation, for they can oppose it only with a weaker dramatisation — weaker because it is conscious of being theatre.

The theatre of individuality is under attack from the techniques that encourage uniformity in a prospering society. Some tried to escape the slums and smoke of the city by taking refuge in a little house whose air was purified by a little green lawn. Soon the suburbs were seen to be slums with air, stifling in spite of it. The rapport with neighbour and nature, apparently off to a new start, again recedes into dream and desire. Now comes the move back into town, to rooms at the top of buildings which, with their flashy luxury, efface the memory (for a month, a year) of the slums of yesterday, the slums outside, below.

Through all the meanderings of collective and individual theatres the group persists, reminder of an unattained rapport, dream of a world where the community can finally

108

be born. The ghettos reappear in replica. Golden ghettos. No one obliges Italians to live together, nor Jews, nor Greeks, nor Poles. It is their free choice. But what is the alternative to the ghetto? Anonymity and marginality. Every large city has its cosmopolitan quarter, colourful and variegated. Tourists in Greenwich Village do not even raise their brows when they see a black woman pass holding a white man's arm, the latter often bearded and dressed to advertise his rejection of society. Here all the minorities gather, of their own free will and in awareness of their condition: sexual, ideological, ethnic minorities. Rebellion, genuine or otherwise, makes of these outcasts a population layer trying desperately, though from beneath, to create some semblance of community; but such a collection of dropouts does not disturb the peace of mind of most ghetto inhabitants. Some of these may even be reassured: those who pretend to choose what is in fact imposed on them. If they so desired they too could join the Bohemians, but, you see, they don't. They are sure Bohemia is a useless masquerade. The ghetto is best: you have comfort and a clear conscience.

Ethnic groups persist because the collective and individual dramatisations of America are now inadequate. They no longer function. But the group is only an absurd reminder of what a community might be. The member of a group can say that he is just as good an American as the next man, that he salutes the same flag and is protected by the same constitution, even if he worships God in his own way and eats some things that are different. There is no need nowadays to be Jewish to enjoy the ritual wine, Manishevitz, and one can eat unleavened bread the year round. Pizza and chop suey have become national dishes, almost on a footing with the hot dog and hamburger. These things, however, only prolong and emphasise the demotion of the group (for non-members) to the status of curiosity or folklore and (for its members) to an object of nostalgia disguised under the tatters of fidelity to a tradition. Every American knows, consciously or not, that individual theatre does not flow into the collective theatre, and that his very belonging to that collective theatre is itself theatrical. Nazism was theatre and folklore, but the German's relationship with his theatre was real. Between him and it there was no distance. Of course his nearness to it was achieved at the price of man's own reality. It is significant that Brecht tried to re-establish distancing in the theatre at the moment when it was eliminated in the colossal theatre of German society.

Ideology does not have this restrictive force in America. When McCarthy tried to apply it, he collided with the individual theatre which Americans would not give up. The tenuousness of American attachment to the collective theatre kept McCarthyism from turning into Nazism (which would have implied a tacit consent on the part of the whole population). It was limited to harrassment by investigators and a kind of petty inquisition.

It must be admitted that American society owes its dynamism to the same contradictions that increasingly paralyse it. If this dynamism is now idling it is because it has produced a degree of material comfort that alienates man from reality. The accumulation of objects does not give a meaning to the world. And the group has its strength in its members' fear of the void. Yet they proclaim their membership with clenched teeth because they know (without admitting the fact to themselves) that the group is not the springboard to a new community but the wretched vestige of an old community condemned to disappear.

The Black is tragically caught in this contradiction; even with a name like White or King, his colour imprisons him in a group whose only reality is the oppression it suffers. An external adversary does not create a sense of communal destiny unless the group has internal resources that give it some cause for hope. The Black sees no hope in America and, looking to Africa, seeks a meaning in his colour. Despair, in an explosion of anger and violence, leads him to take refuge in colour – which finally becomes a true ghetto. In this extremity, the Black dreams of creating a community, of succeeding where white civilisation has failed.

The difficulty experienced by the United States in affirming its place in the world results from the fragility of its theatre and its inaptitude to projection beyond the country's borders. The individual theatre can, of course, be projected as the model for a social structure so dynamic that it fulfills all promises of wealth and comfort. American cars and refrigerators are much admired. Other countries imitate them and arrive in the same impasse. And they rise up against an influence which they might like to accept but are obliged to reject because it comes to them empty-handed, offering only objects, no promise of an escape from history or the human condition the West has forged for man. . . . No dreams? Those America does have for sale, and peddles them shamelessly as such. But Hollywood does not export the millenium.

Europeans like to point out, with a mixture of irritation and malicious glee, that America has nothing but objects to offer the world. They make endless mock of America. Their irritation is the more acute because it is the product of impotence. They themselves do not yet have the utensils that America lavishes on its protégés. They have only words to offer – empty words, because only the masks remain of the theatre they once expressed. Empires have given way under new pressures, and the theatre that gave them coherence has crumbled and become a mockery. England does not even pretend to rule the Commonwealth. At the most she aspires to be a privileged member with rights of seniority. France knows well that it can no longer be the only focal point of Francophone culture, and for lack of means cannot even aspire to be its sole inspiration.

The communist millenium itself has shrunk to an affirmation of Russian power. The West has spent its dreams, and its theatre can no longer serve as a mediation for newly industrialised peoples, for it cannot solve the contradictions of the West itself. Yet the West cannot export its objects and its technology without the dramatic mechanism that made

111

them possible. The occidental theatre becomes a parody when transplanted to former possessions and protectorates. In Accra the parliamentary system becomes a verbal game, and French universality has its faint echo in negritude and communocracy. Parody imposed as theatre quickly becomes a kind of oppression. The chiefs of new African states set up business in former governors' mansions and re-baptise them presidential palaces. Their movements are surrounded with the pomp of an operetta. On great occasions they cast their elites as actors. Their power is no longer magic because they borrow foreign rites. But their subjects are well aware that their new masters cannot establish their authority without using second-hand dramatisations.

This borrowed dramatisation is a weapon against the persistence of direct interference by western dramatisations. The West, its energies exhausted in self-interrogation and contradictions, sees itself opposed by the pale image of its own theatre, caricature of a lost coherence, turned against it by an awaking Orient. We are spectators at a play of phantoms. The East's dilemma is its inability to escape western domination without itself becoming a second-class Occident. Paradoxically, it is discovering western efficiency at the very moment when the West begins to doubt efficiency itself, realising in consternation that it results in the negation of man and ends in an impasse. Moreover, the new countries of the Orient quickly see that the adoption of the theatre of the West does not lead automatically to efficiency, though with the exception of Japan no country has been able to achieve the efficiency of the West without its theatrical machinery. When the West is slapped in the face with a parody of its own theatre, it becomes aware of that theatre's precariousness and fragility, and its doubts become more acute.

Those Europeans who thirty years ago challenged the colonialism practised by their own countries did so in the name of European values. Their particular theatre was somewhat less authoritarian. But it had its domineering elements. Nazism was a tragic, desperate and murderous attempt to renew the theatre of the West. Communism as practiced in Russia became a rigorous, cruel and despotic instrument for appropriating western theatre, and China condemns the USSR, latest recruit to the Occident, in the name of a communism that is oriental. European anti-colonialists of the thirties considered themselves the conscience of the true West and in no way renounced their dream of civilising the East. They were convinced that these primitive peoples needed their help. They devoted themselves to the task with a moral sense that was conscious of its generosity and supremacy. To the moral sense was added, for spice, a touch of curiosity about the exotic aspects of primitive life. The West would perpetuate its influence with clean hands. Nazism, the war, the failure of Communism, and the loss of the western empires deprived western theatre of all foundation. The West no longer feels morally fitted to bring to deprived peoples and cultural orphans a civilisation which may no longer deserve the name. But what if those exotic civilisations had something to offer? What if the primitive peoples held the secret of lost truth? A few little groups in the West set up Zen and other mystico-hygienic curiosities as theatres to replace their own. These, of course, attract only a marginal minority.

The Americans, who with the Russians have taken over the old empires' burden of maintaining the western presence in the Orient, no longer do so in the name of any theatrical coherence. Their projects are without moral base or dramatic justification. Russia has given up the notion of including communism with its exports of weapons and tractors. The Americans have never thought their constitution could serve as a model for other countries. Their exports take the form of dollars, and relate to terms such as development and underdevelopment. Dams are built and gifts of wheat are sent to hungry countries in the hope that these may one day become markets. The West accepts its diminished role and resigns itself to the loss of its civilising mission, though its

113

leaders pretend (with very little conviction) that technological development brings civilisation in its wake. How can they believe it when their own civilisation is going down under the weight of development and technology?

The circle is complete. We return to an era of savages. Conflicts between peoples take place under the sign of violence and barter. The West has lost its coherence, and its theatre has been replaced by nothing. And while we mourn the loss of a dream and, in our mourning, cry out for a new millenium, man, on the verge of a still unformulated Utopia, has not yet come close to the era of the community. He has not reached reality by discarding the theatrical.

Actors and Dictators

To show Egyptians the abuses of which they had been the victims, Nasser's government opened King Farouk's palaces to the public. Visiting one of them I was struck by the almost pathetic anachronism of the luxury it displayed. So that he could enjoy total well-being and wrest a surplus from life (certain as he was that an excess of comfort would provide him with the reality of happiness), the best the Egyptian monarch could do was to buy in Paris boutiques articles that twenty years later had become accessible to every book-keeper and working-girl. Except that Farouk always bought king-size. To say that he had poor taste, that his refinement was middle class, would be to misunderstand what power meant to him. We would likely be more indulgent if he had collected masterpieces or Indian statuettes. Unfortunately the only artistic objects that interested him were pieces of erotic gadgetry.

Farouk belonged to a universe in which power meant more than absolute authority over others: it meant the life overflowing.

Our pity or revulsion at the sight of Farouk's pathetic luxury, intended for use and now reduced to a shabby decor, is matched by our admiration before the heavy beauty of the Chinese drawing-room in Schönbrunn Palace. The fact is that in both cases we are looking at a reality that has turned to folklore, at symbols of a power no longer exercised, at least in the traditional forms to which the symbols refer. The two universes we enter differ only in the distances that separate power from reality. The eastern monarch is a nomad who has arrived in a promised land. His authority accords to him on

115

earth what his subject will taste only in the blessedness of Paradise. The king receives this privilege directly from God, for Islam never divided temporal from spiritual powers. The overflowing life is not obtained by an alliance made with nature in order to enjoy her blessings, but by submitting to God who offers nature as reward. Thus the monarch does not build majestic castles or forts, he does not identify his power with that of the elements and does not symbolise it by mastering nature's resources. Within his palace walls he furnishes a multitude of chambers that allow him to consume life a hundred-fold. These temples of pleasure are ephemeral by their nature. No Arab ruler has left palaces to posterity, except in Spain where western influences were at work. Arab kings consumed life without trying to transform it into a decor.

Schönbrunn impressed me as much as Farouk's palace with its bad taste and air of anachronism. What I mean by bad taste is a beauty that does not well up from reality, a façade that pretends to be real, an artifice that is accepted and admitted as such, an imitation that denies the existence of the original, trickery given preference over direct expression. In Schönbrunn Chinese art is emptied of its substance. The intent of the room was presumably to abolish the distance that separated the essence of the Austrian empire from the craftsmanship of China. The result was simply to embellish part of a palace with a decor that makes the theatrical nature of the whole more obvious. Wealth in this case is not a display from which one has immediate sensual satisfaction. It is the spectacle of the privileges of power that are inaccessible to the monarch's subjects. The sovereign is different through the quality of his decor, not the abundance of his life. Thus the emperor had his permanent box at the Opera. The richness of the Palace decor was accessible only to the privileged few, but the Opera was the place where certain games were played out by a class that pretended to be a faithful interpreter of the whole society. As long as the Empire existed and was powerful these games were not entirely idle. But the moment the decor no longer contains a sovereign who invests himself with appearance in order to acquire reality before his subjects, the decor is hollow. Palace and opera are then open to a public which need not accept the authority these structures represent, for the authority is fictitious. And the structures become tourist attractions.

The Eastern potentate does not have a theatrical relationship to his position of power. His might* is directly expressed. He is butcher, despot, builder of cities. His sensuality is insatiable. Farouk seems to us ridiculous because, lacking the affects of power, the might he deployed was fictitious and became theatrical; an eastern monarch cannot have a theatrical relation with power without appearing foolish. In the West the monarch dramatises his might to make his position of power manifest and render his authority visible. Great Britain has deprived the monarch of all real authority and confined him to the theatre, the pomp and circumstance symbolising power that is exercised by others. In this case it is the theatre which is permanent and the power subject to change. France has attached sovereignty to a general concept. Before the Revolution set up French universality as its theatre, the kings maintained that their authority came from God. In England, where the individual is at the base of the theatrical mediation with reality, the monarch can be reduced to a simple backdrop. In France, on the other hand, because a universal concept gives the theatre its substance, the sovereign is the symbol and custodian of this universality.

Washington goes one stage further in the dramatisation of power. Everyone in London can see the changing of the guard at Buckingham Palace, but they can see very little more. In Washington the public is invited into the White House. In a country where democracy is the mediating

*"La puissance," which is translated here as might, connotes a magnetic inner authority which is self-validating. "Le pouvoir," which refers to the holding of office, is translated variously as power, office, trappings of power, etc. — *Tr.*

notion between the individual and the collectivity, the powers that be adopt this theatrical idea to affirm themselves. The president does not live ostentatiously. He dresses like his inferiors, shakes hands with everyone and displays to the outer world a reassuring austerity. He is very commonplace, and his only obligation is to resemble in an exemplary way an ideal called the average man. He is a faithful husband and a good father. He takes part in public functions and eats undistinguished food. His authority stems from the freely expressed will of the majority of citizens. His reign has a limited duration. What is permanent here is the symbol of the average man holding authority and delegating it to the individual of his choice. It is true that real might belongs neither to the average man nor to his president, but to those who occupy key posts in the financial, industrial and military worlds. But the average man lends his image to this theatre by which might is made manifest and which acts as mediator between the community and the power of the sovereign.

In days when the sovereign was invested with power by hereditary right, he was not haunted by questions about the legitimacy of his authority. It could be challenged by might which did not accept the principle of inherited power, or by legal arguments about lineage. Proponents of such arguments, however, remained pretenders or usurpers until their point was proved. Recognition of authority transmitted by heredity is a recognition that might has its source in life itself. When man's might was still exercised in an animal way and his position of power came from victory and survival in nature, heredity alternated with assassination in the transmission of power.

Mohammed confirmed the choice of those who submitted to the divine will in order to be freed from the hostility of nature. Nature is submissive to the divine will as expressed by its earthly spokesman. On the death of the prophet, Islam was divided on the question of the transmission of power. Is God's will expressed and transmitted through the spirit or through blood relationship? By heredity or election? This fundamental disagreement is still a source of division in Islam. Certain contemporary sovereigns, though they belong to the Sunnite sect, have tried to prove that the blood of the Prophet runs in their veins. Thus the Hashemite family traces its genealogy back to Mohammed, and — a more serious problem for one of Albanian origin — King Farouk paid a historian to establish proof of his direct descendance from the Prophet.

Judaism, unlike Islam, does not mix the function of God's spokesman with that of the leader who does His will. Moses, leader of his people, does no more than write into the law an alliance already sealed in blood between Abraham and his God. Moses is not a perfect man. His destiny is doubtful from the moment of his birth. Is he set afloat in the river so that chance may determine his fate? Does he commit the gratuitous murder of an Egyptian by chance, or in order to document his imperfection? Unlike Mohammed, Moses does not lead his people to war and victory. His path is that of the gradual and tenacious discovery of God's word, which must speak to the heart, the blood and the spirit but is also to be inscribed in stone. From the heights of Mount Sinai the word dominates the world. Reality is thus circumscribed in time and space, and whatever goes beyond the word is exceptional and accomplished by God's special will which is never completely revealed. Moses works miracles because God's will is not limited to the law carved in stone. He is invested with the authority of God, but it is his brother Aaron who is God's spokesman. We can see already how the prophet in Jewish history will establish limits to the king's authority, challenging it constantly. Executive authority can be transmitted by heredity (Solomon was the son of David), but the word of God can be transmitted only by the spiritually elect. The prophet has no family tree.

The western sovereign identifies the conquest of power with the conquest of nature. His role makes him like a wild beast in the forest, leading the pack and having first rights in the prey. His fortress serves as protection against the assaults of enemy packs, and as a refuge in which he can relish the product of the hunt. His formal power extends through space alone, and his might is expressed in his mastery of nature. This mastery is made visible in stone, which the sovereign fashions into a second nature. Might becomes symbolic and his formal power is expressed in this theatre, this second nature created by man's hand. In the safety of his castle the king can claim to be the incarnation of a divine force, but this is only a device to give extra efficacy to his theatre.

As ideology becomes more important the sovereign's role takes on a new form. His might resides in his ability to embody an ideology in its purity, this being the collective theatre by which the group has contact with reality. But as ideology does not extend into the after-life its purity can be challenged, not by new interpretation of a divine word but by the elaboration of another equally coherent system, by the rise of a new theatre which, perhaps only because of its novelty, can be more effective than the old. The religious wars were fairly uniform: purity of doctrine was merely a means of confirming authority or a pretext for challenging it. These wars, along with burnings at the stake and the various inquisitions, were bloody confrontations, ceremonies whose purpose it was to give man a link to the beyond. But the theatre survived this form of mediation. God became a pretext and a hostage in battles between groups. Ideology replaces the theatre of religion, which has lost its power and virtue of mediation. In fact when the Revolution, the Nation, the Race or the Proletariat take the place of God, they are merely patching up a theatre which is falling apart.

The sovereign cannot establish his authority by linking it to the beyond if such a link is meaningless to the group, if religion is no longer the proof of might. The custodian of an ideological truth finds the source of that truth in himself; he need not refer to a supreme and mysterious force, a mighty power from the beyond.

Every ideological upset destroys in its wake a considerable number of purities. Each purity proclaims itself to be unique and pretends to be successor to whatever purity it destroys. When an ideology begins its reign over a society there is only a minute gap between power and might. The man in power demonstrates his might by the very fact that he has assumed his post of authority. To maintain his position he must convince his adversaries and subjects that his might is not a function of the authority conferred on him by ideology. He is a sovereign whose might has its source in ideology, but he must consolidate his power by giving proof of a might that encompasses the ideology itself. Such might gives him the privilege of formulating the articles of his ideology, of interpreting them and modifying them.

Ideological purity does not exist autonomously. It is not inscribed in a code. It becomes an attribute of his person. He maintains himself in power through organised terror, which at the start is simply ideological terror. He creates a gap between formal power and real might. He holds power as the custodian of ideological purity. But in order that the ideology may express genuine might he must relate it to a human community that can accept it as a theatre linking the individual to the collectivity, and this might must at least appear to come from something greater than the collectivity without, however, invoking the beyond. Frequent substitutes for the beyond are "singing tomorrows," or a "better life."

The modern dictator, successor to the king who ruled by divine right, starts from a recognition of collective realities and reduces them to simple ideological formulae in which the group can recognise its hopes and fears. These formulae, through the use he makes of them, become a new reality, a kind of theatre that abolishes the anarchy of reality as experienced, and gives a precise form to an expected future. The image of the future takes on, through this dramatisation, a coherence to which life, with its ambiguities and contradictions, gives the lie every day. Externally the image is not the result of a mere dream, for a flesh-and-blood man assumes and embodies it. This man is endowed with a double power: he symbolises what is possible, and controls the machine that will call it forth from the depth of desire. He is an actor, but the spectacle to which he invites the crowd is not limited by space or time, and pretends to be not a show but rather the movement of life itself. In this sense the dictator has no stage-fright. He does not step knowingly from one world of consciousness into another. He uses his dramatic power not as a mediation with reality nor as a substitute for it, but as reality itself.

The moment of stage-fright has always seemed to me to be precisely the one in which the actor leaves reality to make his plunge into the theatrical. It is a moment of intense clarity of feeling in which the artist leaves life behind: he inhabits the territory of death for a second before being rescued by the birth of his role. The degree of control with which he makes this transition from reality to theatre is the measure of his talent and of the depth of his sensitivity. The mechanisation of this phenomenon is a technique which eliminates the always unpredictable involvement of emotions, the vibrations of life.

Without even having to appear in public the dictator can exploit the distance between theatre and reality, and himself incarnates the might which can eliminate the gap. The gap in fact remains, but he brings about an acceptance of present reality by means of a theatre which he presents as the future, a future he has the might to determine, an ineluctable future that is first greeted as a hope and then imposed in the form of terror, even after it has been exposed as a fraud. The dictator is a second-rate actor, or rather one who is consciously and basically dishonest. He may well be the victim of his own fraud. But for him the theatre is only a means which he uses to shore up his authority, as God was a means for his predecessor the king. His theatre does not transform reality, but he must pretend that it does; and those who express doubt about the transformation, those who still believe in the coming of a reality his theatre gave glimpses of, are anathema to his system. They are traitors who must be eliminated.

Western sovereigns nowadays push the exploitation of the theatrical to extremes in their struggle to come to power. Might is not expressed in imitations of nature. Rulers no longer live in castles or indulge in luxurious display. The police and the army ensure the acceptance of a kind of might whose only substance is theatrical: the ideology or, in its place, a general idea of the world or of the people to be governed. The modern sovereign separates his person from the theatre he exploits, by a gap which is perceptible only to himself. When he has grasped power he uses the police mechanism to retain it, pretending to be the custodian of legitimacy, with an ideology or key concept to back him up.

Napoleon provides us with one of the first examples of the sovereign who bases his authority on ideology and retains it for the simple reason that he was able to seize it in the first place. The effectiveness of the Revolution's ideology sputtered out in the succession of conflicting purities that a series of custodians imposed by terror. Napoleon was able to give this ideology a semblance of reality, a permanence and concrete substance: France. The Revolution was no longer an idea or a dream, it was a fatherland. What allowed Napoleon to establish the necessary distance, the free play between himself on the one hand and France and the Republic on the other — the detachment of the actor from the role he plays — was the fact that he was neither a revolutionary nor a Frenchman. He used his authority to give substance to his own might, building an empire and basing the legitimacy of his power not on the theatre of the Revolution but on a real Empire.

It was in Austria that Hitler developed the general concept of Germany and the Aryan race, as he himself recounts in *Mein Kampf*. He achieved an actor's objectivity toward the power he was to pursue and capture. Technology allowed him to extend and amplify the theatrical relationship between his own magnetic influence and his formal powers.

It was through radio that he built his role. He was meticulous about the settings of his public appearances: arriving deliberately late, he knowingly built a suspense to which he then gave an outlet. His presence was marked by flags, streamers and torchlight parades. His party troops were uniformed, though they belonged to neither police nor army. Later, Hitler was to consolidate his might through an elaborate police mechanism, and try to perpetuate it by establishing an empire. But he never ceased to justify both police and empire in the name of the general concept, the theatre which gave Germans their cohesion and their mediation with nature.

The only music Stalin genuinely enjoyed was the folk music of Georgia. A filter in his emotional makeup separated him from the Russians and all the other national groups that made up his empire. Like Napoleon and Hitler he was able to give an ideology its fatherland; the dream of a classless society became a Russian hope. The ideological theatre he imposed through his police power was more than a swindle: it was oppression. Thus, when the Germans penetrated his defences, Stalin appealed to an older, more traditional cohesion: that of the land. This was all the more effective in that the idea of Russia had a fresh reality for a people whose armies were being driven back. During the war his might was expressed not in Marxist terminology but in Russian words. As an actor he had the detachment needed to switch easily from role to role, first as father to the proletariat and then as emperor of all the Russias.

It was in London that de Gaulle conceived his role as saviour of France. The "certain idea" which he had of France could not help but raise a humiliated people and encourage them to surpass themselves. De Gaulle gave the French an enlargement of their country. His country was a grandiose theatre on whose stage it was normal to see men and women forgetting their everyday roles. De Gaulle had such an irresistible vision of himself as mediator between reality and theatre that he spoke of himself in the third person. He

124

consciously saw himself playing a role on a majestic stage: that of History.

In his *Philosophy of Revolution* Nasser tried to become the mediator between a double collective theatre (Arab and Islamic) and a reality which he was attempting to transform. The Islamic countries did not conceive of themselves as parts of a general Islam, and disliked the notion of transforming religion into a collective theatre. Nasser was also unable to obtain the support of Arabs as such for his total program. To achieve cohesion among Egyptians he spoke of socialism. This was, of course, an ideological dramatisation and not a program of action. Here again he ran into resistance from facts and men. It was not an Egyptian solution to have as leader a man who, instead of using his position of power to express his own might, attempted to act as mediator between an unbearable reality and a theatre he had invented. Egypt is still too close to the living sources of the Semitic East to tolerate such an arrangement. The might of their sovereign is expected to be visible, and his power should be exercised so as to bring him the concrete benefits of luxury and riches. Nasser, unsuccessful in maintaining his power through a western kind of theatre, had no choice: he had to fall back on a traditional source of power, the army. But when the army becomes more than a simple instrument in the hands of an unequivocally mighty sovereign, its power is ephemeral and its theatrical effects inoperative.

Technology allows the West to push the dramatisation of power to new extremes. Television reduces the sovereign to an image, and his might to the attraction he can exercise over a multitude of viewers. It is no longer the man who is invested with power, but his shadow. John Kennedy made good use of his charm and won over many viewers with his quality of youthful dynamism. His electors identified with the free vibration of life in his bearing. His wealth was not a reward obtained through the exercise of power but a key to gaining it. A millionaire, young and happy, model husband

125

and father, he had nothing material to gain from power. He could exercise it with supreme detachment.

Once elected, to be sure, Kennedy demonstrated other qualities. He arbitrated between opposing forces. He administered might that was not his own, and of which he was not even the custodian. One man is no longer expected to embody might, and an American president is elected because of the borrowed personality he radiates. He may be re-elected if, in this new role of actor, he does not confuse power and might.

Great ambiguity surrounds the role of heads of state in democratic countries. People vote for them if the personality they project is attractive. They are damned if they appear weak, and damned if they aspire to might. They are, in fact, expected to occupy a happy middle ground between anarchy and dictatorship, with the understanding that they are open to reproach for indecisiveness and lack of a clear conception of their role.

Modern technology manufactures numerous, inter-changeable and often highly imprecise images of leaders, and the spectator becomes the arbiter within his own theatre. He himself is mighty; he can endow a leader with power or deprive him of it. But this might is itself theatrical, for the economic and technological forces that govern the disposition of power are beyond the grasp of the average man.

Thus elector and elected play their game together. Real might is deaf, mute and blind, and public power is not the path that leads to it. Sovereign and subjects take part in a theatre which has no mediating function. The alternative is the arbitrary use of might; but in the age of technology no man can make his own sovereign might a credible thing. The theatre that used to link positions of power with might has lost its effectiveness, and real might seems something distant and absurd. It can no longer impose on men an arbitrary fate, for the will of the gods is no longer recognised. And might which can never be taken in hand seems itself to be theatrical. One cannot submit to it without feeling oppressed,

126

and when one submits the oppression becomes insidious and pervasive. Enemies are needed, and if they cannot be found they are invented. For might does not disappear. It becomes an absurd oppression when the mediations leading to it have gone inoperative. Man, caught between an illusory liberty and an intangible oppression, vents his rage and impotence in violence or collapses into resignation.

The Word and the Place

In their oscillations between perpetual nostalgia and the loss of some portion of themselves, few voluntary exiles recover entirely from their banishment. I chose to leave one civilisation and adopt another: one more individual adventure, obscured or diminished to the vanishing-point in the total flood of immigrants.

No one can change the language he speaks, the bread he eats, the colour of his sky, without his very substance being thrown into confusion; without his newly vulnerable being revealing its secrets; without his mystery, ignored until now because taken for granted, being exposed in all its fragility. Very few are able to resist. One begins to search for any kind of new security, even if one must settle for no more than the surface of old certainties. The voluntary exile must forget who he is, and pretend to follow a rhythm out of phase with his own. Otherwise he isolates himself — though the isolation is mitigated by a new everyday life — within his own secret, living out in exile a diminished reality composed of nostalgia and rites or customs that seem more and more anachronistic. He has no choice but to forget himself, if he wants to live out his fate completely and not avoid it. He is a shared, a divided man, who finds in his distress a new balance that brings with it energy and richness greater than all those blindly given by a rooted existence.

In the anonymity of his own collectivity he does not think about his identity: is it anything more than his surname, his work, his family status? Transplanted, these things are not indications of belonging, they are symbols of difference. I am not speaking of those who are obliged by

128

political or economic circumstances to leave their country and make a new start elsewhere; or rather I speak only of those among them who attempt to turn a forced exile into a choice, opting consciously not for a new anonymity, nor for a useless and illusory fidelity to their past, but for a division of their being.

Lived to the full this choice takes a modern man along a path quite different from those of anonymity or the putting down of roots. Is this path a new hope? Success is uncertain and the rewards fragile. We are talking about a process, a state of mind, an openness to life, not about a mechanism with predictable consequences.

If I exile myself voluntarily I consciously put myself in a vulnerable state. The resulting torment is my way of rejecting emptiness, of recreating my being in risk and danger. If I put my most private self on the line it is perhaps so that I may remain aware of it, so that it does not imperceptibly disappear. First to be risked is the mirror of my privacy: my means of expression.

Changing one's language means more than mastering a new one. I can be perfectly polyglot in my own country; on trips or visits abroad I can converse in languages far removed from my own. Then other languages are a kind of knowledge that opens doors for me, vehicles that make exchanges possible. That has nothing to do with my decision to make a foreign language my primary tool of expression. The effects are profound, even though they are imperceptible at the beginning.

I learned French in Baghdad. But I wrote in Arabic, and saw myself already as one of the artisans of a literary revival in my country. French, a foreign tongue, opened new and liberating horizons. World culture seemed to be within my reach. In Paris this language became an instrument for daily use, an immediate and natural fact. Without my realising it, the field of my mother-tongue shrank. Arabic was kept for conversations with my countrymen. Speaking French all day long, I was furious when I had to speak it with a classmate from Baghdad because we happened to be with a Frenchman. In our native city this would have been a simple matter of courtesy. In Paris it was a revelation of the change in value that our language had undergone. It was now a distant, exotic phenomenon. Only when I was writing — in Arabic — did I rediscover my private world and feel completely myself again. I wrote about my new city, I wrote about the French. Now I could reverse the situation: it was the French who were exotic creatures requiring explanation. I rediscovered the complicity of words. A public that I could imagine was there before my eyes. I was no longer in Paris, or at least only temporarily, on some kind of errand. As I wrote I reoccupied my own universe, I won back my country word by word.

The attraction of France was too great: I could not succumb to the enticements of exile. I now tried to reverse the earlier process: I wanted to communicate in French what was nearest to my heart, to translate to the West my reality as an Oriental. But we cannot switch languages without a revolution in our inner life. To possess the French language and live within it, to manipulate it from the inside meant a total change in my rapport with reality. Certain images were ineradicable. And gross mistakes that persisted despite a long apprenticeship denoted the survival of a vision of the world that I had consciously and voluntarily traded for another. Even if I no longer say *le lune* or *la soleil,* the sun for me remains inalterably the sun of my childhood: it belongs to the feminine kingdom, and the moon to the masculine. Arabic and French are poles apart in the relationships they establish with reality. Arabic, a language in which conceptualisation is a borrowed function, makes no use of the adjective because it is foreign to its genius. Arabic is the language of the thing named, not the thing qualified. The image replaces the adjective, and when an adjective is used it never has the precision it possesses in languages derived from Greek or Latin.

I came to French encumbered by the heavy baggage of Arabic. French was a fragile instrument which I could at any moment either transform by the magic of another language, or bury under a florid style. From this time on I explored the tortuous ways of my own language like a French tourist, with a learned but imprecise air, for my new precision was borrowed. Writing in two languages had become an impossibility. I lived simultaneously in two worlds, with a resultant tension that at times was intolerable, occasionally beneficial. To write in two languages without one becoming an echo or reflection of the other would have required a useless effort I was not prepared to make. I no longer lived in the Orient, because I refused to consider myself an exile in France. The old world I bore within me, but I felt free in the new, because as soon as I succeeded in making it my own it became a second reality for me. I saw no further need to write in Arabic. I could no longer struggle against my need to live in the French universe. But on what conditions could I live there? At this moment my real emigration began. Pressures were there, and increasing: should I change my name, never again speak Arabic, declare myself haughtily and proudly occidental, consign the Orient to oblivion or contempt? It was out of respect for the world I was entering that I wanted to preserve what was most precious from my former world, the direct access to intimacy. One can only change languages in full awareness of what is involved, measuring what is left behind, what has been abandoned. Otherwise there is no change of language, merely a change of the vehicle of conversation. One does not immigrate from one culture to the other, though one can move from one city to another.

Avoiding the tensions would have led to a loss of self. Only in tension can one hew out a place in the new language, this unknown land that the explorer alters as he discovers it, making of it not a stopover or an invisible decor, but an inhabited place. Languages cannot be superimposed nor do they cohabit separately. They grow together: one invades the

131

other, informs the other, pressing it from within to the bursting point. The separate man who chooses and accepts his separateness ends by living beneath a double mask, and a mask does more than protect integrity and privacy against intruders; it also raises a screen between man and reality. The division of his being, once accomplished, forces him into theatre. He welcomes a new world effusively in order to make tolerable an existence which he does not really choose, and at the same time he idealises a previous world in which he no longer believes, even if he convinces himself that he will one day return to it. The dilemma of the divided man is that he becomes accustomed to living in a double dramatisation, and even when he returns to his native country it no longer seems real to him; it becomes bearable only if it is transformed in turn to a stopover in relation to his second world, and embellished by nostalgia as is every theatrical universe.

In Montreal *le genièvre hollandais* becomes *du gros gin,* and if oranges from Baghdad were imported to this city they would lose their savour. The traveller delights in the surprises of foreign tastes, but this is inverted homesickness, for he reassures himself by dreaming of the certainties of his national cuisine. If in his home city he seeks out from time to time the exotic dishes of other countries, it is by his own choice, and he has no need to abandon or modify his relationship with the products of nature.

When I was in Baghdad the insistence of western poets on the beauties of springtime seemed to me a little exaggerated. Even lyricism and imagination, I thought, should have a limit. Our fruit was not imported, and when friends coming back from vacations in the north brought us the over-sized peaches that grew there, we knew that what we were tasting was foreign and did not belong to our world. And when I passed a store frequented by the foreign colony (mainly British), overflowing with European fruit, tinned food, spices and delicatessen products, I knew there was no point in my crossing the threshold. These things were not intended for me. One day, tired of knowing the West through books alone, and wanting to experience the smell of it, I entered as though going on a voyage. I never went back. I hadn't been after a change of scene, nor some exotic thrill, and I found in this fraction of Europe only doors that opened on unreality.

Later I knew the sea, the rains of summer, springtime, snow. . . . I was always tempted to take refuge in the relativity of seasons and climates, with the desert and its scorching heat as my yardstick in the diversity of nature, so that another sky might seem more pure, another climate less hostile. But one has not yet left a country if it remains the measure for all others. To emigrate is to tear oneself deliberately away from immediate reality and the external world, without turning nature into a stage-set. To emigrate is to plunge consciously into a new winter, a different summer, to forget the taste of fruit only to discover it again, to die in order to live again, to bury one life in memory so that another can flower. Then nature loses its innocence. From that moment our reaction to it ceases to be instinctive. It is a learned reality, discovered, autonomous. Now we know that spring exists because we have experienced its absence. And we do not take the plunge in innocence, for we do not live in immediate intimacy with nature and its relativity, but in a series of deaths and rebirths. I know now that it is possible to live without having experienced the desert, or without mountains, or without snow. But the earth is not a fatherland that we carry in our hearts, nor is it a changing backdrop. On it we live out our death and our birth, our fragility and our permanence, approaching but never reaching the promised land of a marriage of man and nature. If the external world is not to become theatre, each tree, each fruit, each season is final and unique, and I must tear myself away from the familiar, transform myself by changing worlds, lose myself, find myself again, accumulating successive realities without confusing them.

133

When we are no longer tempted to set ourselves over against nature in order to protect our autonomy, home becomes possible; a city is no longer a stopover. Jerusalem is the city of perpetual desire, Rome the dwelling place of a church and Mecca a rallying point and pilgrim's goal. There have been many attempts to transform a particular spot into a chosen place where man will surpass himself, a place that is not a symbol but an incarnation, a station for what is transcendant. One can go anywhere in the world bearing a new Jerusalem. One can carry forever the sign of a visit to Mecca, home of the last prophecy. Pilgrims there complete their religious duty by touching the sacred place with their foot. They are transformed, and their privileged relationship with nature is not an ephemeral moment but a stage in their total journey, one that transforms them by transforming their link with earth. They have known the sacred place in their own flesh, and nature takes on a new aspect. From now on they bear the name of Hadj, and nature is real because it is sanctified by their pilgrimage. The mystical union is accomplished, and they need no longer live in expectancy. To become master of the soil the pilgrim must cross the desert, so that reality is not transcended but mastered, so that nature ceases to be the constant temptation of the sacred.

The temple of Jerusalem never gave a fixed point to hope nor put an end to waiting. Jerusalem is the city of the marriage of man and space, to be accomplished only in the future; but the wait cannot be abandoned without loss of self, without inevitable exile and pilgrimage.

Rome is a consecration of the full stop; it is the acceptance of a nature that cannot be transcended while we are within it, of a city which is merely the stage where life is played, a place of transients (since real life cannot exist in space, in a fixed and visible location). Rome is the end of the long wait, it is resignation to the divorce of man from reality, the consummation of his separation; it is theatre triumphant.

Coming from the desert to the plenty of Europe, from absence to presence, the place was not for me a physical thing to be taken for granted, but a discovery and an acquisition. We cannot possess a place, but we can tame it in a transitory way. The choice is re-opened every moment. The place exists because it changes us; if it does not it is mere decor and we are in exile. The Orient, which denies the place, sanctifies it in compensation. Sanctification is a victory over exile, and I learned this on the shores of the West, where nature could be neither a decor nor a stopover. I learned to sanctify place to make it livable, but to my surprise it grew habitable independently of me, offering its blessings, its wealth, its beauties and colours, generously and of its own accord. Yet this autonomy of place can send me back into exile as easily as any hostility or desolation of place. I have to earn my own locale, I must win my home and merit it. If a change of place is not to be merely an exchange of one kind of exile for another, I must inhabit my home fully, make every minute sacred. This real link with place is the living experience that conducts us to the sacred. I am present at the creation of the world, but am not and cannot be a mere spectator. The world is not a theatre, I am participating in its creation. This is the poetic act, but it is also the negation of poetry. The conquest of each moment, the creation of place, is the living experience called poetry, a continuous invention; and yet by the same token any expression of the moment, of the sacred, becomes empty, exhausted in the very process of consummation.

I change cities. One succeeds the other, not super-imposed but contesting one another. If I resist the tempta-tion of exile it is at the price of comfort, external harmony, any obvious concord. My habitation is in dispute, and I occupy tensions which must each day be overcome; each day I must admit that the place has no reality unless I create it at every moment. I can no longer enjoy a relaxed and innocent rapport, from the moment a new place puts the first in question. And the new place itself is challenged, for now I must live in it with my eyes open. I choose it, and must constantly rebuild and reconstitute it. Otherwise the chal-

135

lenges drive me to escapism, to the refuge of exile, or to the annihilation of the real place by the absence of all links between us.

I have known the desert and the great wastes of snow, and for me the desert and the snowy wastes have forever lost their innocence.

I belong to a contested minority. I have lived in the shadow of great civilisations. Some were falling apart, others were in the throes of creation, founding themselves on disagreement with that relationship to reality which my minority has never wholly achieved, but which it has always persisted in pursuing. My minority, in spite of itself, has become a reminder and a hope.

Islam rode through the world bearing witness with the sword and the word. It accepted the survival in its midst of a different vision of hope, that of the Jews: a vision well-developed and vibrant enough to open the possibility of a challenge, but too feeble for the challenge to be real or do more than confirm the majority in its rights and certainties.

At the end of my adolescence, on the threshold of manhood, I discovered Christianity. I could at any time have protected my contested humanity by clothing myself in this foreign exoticism. I also knew the Arab minority, one not unlike my own, which lived first as a challenge to Christianity and then defensively, searching for inner strength with which to combat the western attempt to still its feeble, persistent voice, its reminder, plaintive but insistent and indomitable, of a lack, a non-achievement, an absence. I was able to compare Islam with Christianity only on the basis of the relation each has with Judaism, which has itself become a private consciousness, and an unhappy one. Here again I found myself in a minority, but this time on my own terms, for I was twice outnumbered: once by Christianity and again by western Judaism, which has perhaps not changed its attitude of expectancy, but has indeed changed its dream, giving a different resonance to its will, a different colour to its obstinacy.

Thus the West opposed me doubly and exercised a double temptation: to lose myself in a despised minority, or simply to lose myself. Then came the long apprenticeship of a strange language and the weight of unfamiliar words; and then, the discovery of relationships with humans, suddenly fully present for me because of my need to take note of them, if only in profile.

As a child, speaking to the Moslems of my own city, in their dialect rather than my own, I had a forewarning of what it was to belong to a minority, and I refused to accept that condition. I had to give way to the majority, hide the light of my way of speech, and adopt that of others in order to come closer to them, speaking to them on their terms, willing to forego the need for equality, as one must in any true exchange. My faith was my secret, and a secret need only be shameful for it to become a shackle.

Finally I refused to hide my origin and reject my dialect. I did not want my relationship with the majority to be established at the expense of the idea I had of myself. The more this idea became conscious, the more decisive it was for me. Gradually this lucid awareness seemed to me a privilege, and my weakness became a strength. The one who addressed me knew that I was different, that I was the foreigner. But I not only knew that he was the Other, I also knew that he saw in me the foreigner. This was the advantage I had over him: an indirect rapport that was consciously doubled back. Would he oblige me to play the role he had assigned to me? This is where the Orient I carry in me comes to the surface, and acquires the weight of consciousness. Western man has been schooled by his theatre. For centuries he has been perfecting the division of his personality. Between him and the one who addressed him, dialogue was at first established tortuously. The member of a minority had to accept his condition and recognise the privileged position of the other by adopting his way of speech. After centuries of conceptualisation it was easy to raise a screen between speakers, to separate them from their origins, until each came to consider himself as member of a majority, taking care to meet the Other only on neutral ground where each could maintain the idea he had of himself, revealing to the other only a facade. Theatre became the neutral ground where each man accepted the death of his self in the presence of others, in order that he might keep the secret which was his breath of life.

Politeness became a safe-conduct for crossing the zone that separated reality from theatre. There was no need to change facial expressions, for the real face was masked. Dissimulation became quite unconscious. It was merely one aspect of the theatre that pervaded and replaced life.

I was used to greater frankness, but also to a real dissimulation. In the Orient, because the rapport between man and reality is not theatrical, one looks for relationships that are direct and not oblique, though in full awareness that they are unattainable. And when one has recourse to theatre, it is not as a system on which to base a world-view but as a mechanism, a subterfuge, an instrument that must be spontaneously invented. If passions, despite their violence, seem ephemeral in the Orient, it is because they are not confined within a system of mediation which would formal-ise them and rob them of their spontaneity (while constantly feeding them). In the Orient passions succeed each other, like fidelities, and renew themselves. Though they may lack constancy they do not lose their reality. There may be dissimulation, but each face keeps its character and becomes its living self again at the first opportunity. It dons successive states. It is multiple, unpredictable. One cannot rely on any theatrical consistency, for this face is touched at every moment by the movement of life, a movement that is unpredictable and uncontrollable.

My self-division in the Orient was a ruse borrowed by passion for its own survival. The face changes colour so as not to go inert. This changing face that refuses the mask of death in fact makes death draw back. Speaking the Moslems' dialect, I merely muted one passion in order to participate in another – but now on my own conditions. And I always

138

ended up deep in the game, for all consciousness would have been impotent if the motor of my behaviour had been a concentration on the immobility of death, rather than life in its iridescence.

In the West I discovered politeness and lucidity. I discovered theatre. Here self-division was not a succession of facial expressions; it was more basic. It affected my relationships with others and my rapport with reality. What for me had been a game, an improvisation, spontaneity, became a system, an instrument of survival. What had been freedom and a ruse of life became an enslavement, self-abandonment, resignation to death. I knew now that my Eastern theatre in occidental eyes meant duplicity and hypocrisy, that what was transitory was seen as frivolity. The iridescence of life was here suspect.

I changed my language and my vision of reality was overturned. Then suddenly in some oriental restaurant, I would hear a recording of Arab music and the forgotten world was there again, for an instant as well-defined and terminal as parentheses. What had been a natural part of life became a dream, a contrived atmosphere. At any cost I had to avoid the trap of homesickness, to save what for me remained my true rapport with reality. Then there was the little group of compatriots whom I could isolate and abstract from the world around. With them I would speak my own language avidly, with the pleasure of a lost gift recovered, a skill buried and found again. But this was yielding to the temptations of exile; and were not homesickness and exile precisely the theatre the Orient could not accept without denying itself and dying inwardly — the theatre the West had systematised so well?

I had to make the attempt to guard the Orient from exile and homesickness, but without artificial distractions. It was a rescue operation, but the rapport with reality that was to be rescued had not yet been established. It was still in the realm of desire. And in any case direct rapport with reality had to be lived in its own locale. Transplanted, it became

139

theatre. I found myself plunging headfirst into the dilemma: recapture the Orient and protect myself from western theatre; yet also experience the West completely without embracing its divisions and dichotomies. Two ways were open to me. I could try to transform the West, approach it on my own terms, as if it were new and made no stipulations. But this was too ambitious; it overestimated my strength and underestimated the true dimensions of the West. Or I could lodge the Orient within me, make it a personal realm, neither dream nor illusion but a private place where the rapport with reality could become an immediate presence, a disposition to spontaneity. In other words, the Orient could become the domain of poetry. What was no longer open to me in daily life might be possible in moments of heightened intensity.

But daily life has its own power. I move among beings whose life is single, unique as it may be. I envy them, while pitying their poverty. My own life is twofold, or can be. But at what a price! I know that I am different and the others know I am conscious of my difference. This game of "I know that you know that I know" can be prolonged indefinitely, precisely because it is a game. To be foreign and conscious of it in no way diminishes the anguish of absence. The great dilemma is to be present and to accept being different.

Are we not all *marranos*?* At some point in our lives we carefully hide the thing that gives our existence its very weight and substance. We shield our secret from hostile eyes. And we are ashamed of it. Exile is a refuge, a safe harbour that allows us to practise virtue in a world busy erasing it. Exile could be sweet if it were no more than the tribute I pay a hostile world, one that forces me to live in pretended harmony with reality. Yet refusing exile, obliged to lead a diminished life, I am no less concerned about substance and reality. I talk to those around me and it is an act of rescue:

---

*In the days of the Inquisition, Spanish Jews who were forced to become converts to Catholicism but continued to practise their own religion in secret were called by the Spaniards *marranos*, the hideous ones. (*Tr.*)

these shadows in a weightless world are lit up by my concern. A part of myself becomes theirs, and already we are in communion. Their world is mine. They grasp this fact. What perturbation have I brought into these lives, that never before questioned their own validity? My tensions become theirs, and now it is they who prefer exile, taking refuge in their certainties. I violate their quiet, I overturn their private worlds. I am no longer the foreigner but the intruder. What a temptation now to retreat to the warmth of my own ghetto! My exile would become attractive, I could endow it with all the attributes of autonomy, I could have a separate life and the illusion of a full one. No one chooses tension cavalierly, and it is the need for peace and the warmth of certainties that drive the foreigner to become a *marrano*. How can I abandon my certainties without shaking those of others? One cannot exchange a set of certainties for another without living in a shadow universe. But I can become a *marrano* only as a last resort, out of my own cowardice or that of others. Then I will pretend to share the certainties of the new society while jealously safeguarding my own. I will accept a world of unreal appearance. Theatre is at work, and sets up its screen between myself and others when I need and seek a link with them. The breath of life becomes a secret cult, presence and absence are blurred, and death has the upper hand.

I must crack the walls protecting others, make them realise that they too are strangers, foreigners, arouse doubt where there was certainty, make complacent men admit that the foreigner is not merely the Other, the one who has come from another place, and that their own place can change its nature through the presence of the stranger if he is not pushed back into sham and pretence, if he himself does not accept the notion of exile. Only in this way can I overcome the condition of *marrano*. To those I trust, I open the strangeness and novelty of natural place, for I confer upon it the sacred character of presence. And we succeed together in living certain privileged moments, brief, dangerous, exacting and forbidding. Suddenly reality seems not to be a certainty

141

but something that must be won through an incessant struggle. We succeed only by living two lives. We know, if only unconsciously, that these moments of freedom and abandon, these extensions of all our individual lives into those of others, will be followed by long hours in which we will be alone and will have to prepare a place for our solitudes; hours when the paths of exile, relativity and absence will lie before us as constant temptations. We will have to pass through the strait gate — the waiting and ancient hope — while realising that we all lead double lives, and that, if we persist in rejecting the theatrical, we must resign ourselves to being torn by our inner division. One moment I am with others; in the next, I am the stranger to them. In rhythmic alternation we are close, then strangers, and in this balancing act our equilibrium is re-established; our rapport with reality is not theatrical because we turn our backs on exile and *marranism*. The distance that rules each of my gestures toward the Other does not separate me from him, for it is born continually of alternation. If I accept the fact of being divided between communion and the ancient hope, it is because I reject the division of being, I refuse to live simultaneously in two worlds. My two universes are not superimposed. They continue each other, prolong one another in the movement that is life. Though my relationship with reality is conscious, it is not frozen by a lucidity of awareness that rules out adventure or chance. Alternation within continuity is creation; and my rapport with others is not a closed achievement but an eternal starting-point. I have opted for a language which I must invent as I speak. I have chosen a place which I endow with presence by inscribing my invention upon it. I have chosen a rapport with others which, far from imprisoning them in their own language or in a fixed place not of their choosing, draws them into a movement where language, place and the Other are invented every moment, obliging me to invent myself. I do not accept the fixity of safe places or the comfort of certitudes.